HOW TO ZING!
YOUR LIFE AND
LEADERSHIP

21 INSIGHTS ON
MAXIMIZING YOUR INFLUENCE

NANCY HUNTER DENNEY

D1373854

Viaticum Press
Mason, Ohio

Published by Viaticum Press in Mason, Ohio

Cover Design by Dawn Teagarden
Typesetting by Jonathan Gullery

To Order Books or Inquire about Group Sales:
www.zingbook.com or call: 888.566.7536

Distributed by:
Potential Leadership Training and Lectures
49 South Street – Suite 1041
Marion, MA 02738
888.566.7536

Library of Congress Cataloging-in-Publication Data

Denney, Nancy Hunter, 1960-
    Includes Bibliographical references.
    How to *Zing!* Your Life and Leadership: 21
    Insights on Maximizing Your Influence/ Nancy
    Hunter Denney
    LCCN: 2004095534

ISBN 0-9631834-6-X
1. Leadership. 2. Motivation. 3. Business.
I. Denney. Nancy Hunter. II. Title.

Printed in the United States of America

*This book is dedicated to those who have the insights to seek
happiness, play in the rain, love their family and friends,
show grace in the face of adversity, follow their heart,
believe in the power of prayer, value what they have while they
have it;
and make the world a better place just by being in it…*

*For my life and leadership, I dedicate this book to
my loving husband, Tom, precious children, Kaitlin and Jake, dear
parents, Rosalie and Chip Hunter, and to my favorite mother-in-law,
Edith Denney.
With special dedication to
my incredible sisters, Barbara Quinn, Elizabeth Price,
and Gabrielle Miller—women of many insights.*

CONTENTS

FOREWORD

You are going to find great enjoyment, direction, and *Zing!*, in reading this book. It provides an immediate positive charge to your attitude and outlook on life, because it is packed with the punch of collective voices spoken by one dedicated educator, and difference maker. If you want to take your life and leadership to higher levels, this book will teach you not only why, but how to override competing forces to positively influence others.

How to Zing! Your Life and Leadership is a practical guide for individuals dedicated to making the world a better place, one person, company, neighborhood, or organization, at a time. In a unique approach, Nancy Hunter Denney has studied ideas, principles, laws, practices, and even a few fish tales, from leadership and motivational experts around the country to arrive at twenty-one insights necessary for *Zing!* – a term she uses to symbolize positive influence, energy, and charisma.

Whether for personal, family, community, or professional use, the anecdotes and examples provided in this book will hit a personal cord. Nancy speaks directly to you – the reader – as if you were seated next to her. Her optimism in the future is apparent, as is her challenge to your leadership and life potential.

Throughout every page, Nancy asks tough questions, tells great stories, and guides you down a path of higher character, happiness, and clarity of purpose. With this understanding you can plant positive seeds of hope, love, encouragement, and faith.

As a result of reading *Zing!* you will be encouraged to not only live your life for a greater good, but will possess the most significant tools needed to start, re-direct, or continue your work. Nancy has given you literally hundreds of tips, skill-building lessons, and opportunities for self-introspection, designed to jump start more productive attitudes and behaviors.

God has given us all special gifts, but they are not for us alone.

Our gifts are meant to bless the lives of others, and that's what making a difference is about. My friend, Nancy Hunter Denney, has done a *super-fantastic* job of discussing leadership as the process of making a difference. Enjoy.

—Keith Harrell

ACKNOWLEDGEMENTS

I don't think it's possible to write a book by yourself. The words in this book may have come from my laptop, but they were influenced by many insights shared unselfishly with me over my lifetime. I want to thank my closest friends; Sue Serrato, Jen Roberts, Linda Quinlavin, Jean Urbanowski, Kristy Barnes, Karen Matt, and Stacey Stimets. I also want to thank those dedicated professionals who have inspired me to seek higher standards of life and leadership; Mrs. Anderson, Ms. Sue Campinha, Ms. Jane Root, Mr. Jim Carlson, Ms. Kate Calise, Mrs. Belsito, Mrs. Kiritsy, Mrs. Mary Kate Soter, Dr. Judy Robinson, Dr. Ralph Iannuzzi, Dr. Robert Maloney, Ms. Diane Willis, Ms. Kari Eisenhooth, Mr. Denny Faurote, Dr. Will Keim, Mr. Marlon Smith, Dr. Dennis Black, Dr. Maureen Hartford, Mrs. Jane Tesso, Dr. Susan Salvador, Mrs. Janet Richardson, Mr. Bernie Brown, Rev. Jim Rand, and Rev. Bob MacFarlane.

Appreciation is extended to the following individuals who excel in their area of expertise; Dave Fortin of Media Image Productions, Mo Bowen of Sisters, Dawn Teagarden of Teagarden Designs, James Malinchak of James Malinchak International, and Joyce Soares of Seaver Printing.

Finally, enormous amounts of thanks are extended to my editor, Elisa Lorello, whose spirit, faith and excitement for this project kept me on task.

INTRODUCTION

ZING! IS THE THING!

Would you hang out with you if you didn't have to? Is your life beige? Now is the time to fill all aspects of your life with the color of *Zing!*.

WHAT IS "ZING!"?

Zing! is your *ability to override competing forces to positively influence others towards a greater social good.* *Zing!* is about influencing others to make the world a better place while maximizing your potential for a more successful, happier and more productive life. *Zing!* begins with you and ends with others. *Zing!* is what you get when you add the letter "z" to the word "charisma" and add an exclamation point. With *Zing!* you will find yourself more confident in your abilities to achieve your goals. With enhanced confidence comes enhanced opportunity. Regardless of your goals in life, being more influential (or *"charizmatic"*) allows you to replace the shadows and darkness in your life with light.

No more complaining that you were once again passed up, passed by, overlooked, undervalued, or "screwed over." No more settling. No more self-defeating language, victim mentality, or boredom. It's time for a kick in the seat of your pants, a jolt between the ears, and for you to put a bounce back in your step. The insights offered in this book will lead you directly to the light switch; all you have to do is turn it on!

Based on the idea "wherever you go, there you are," *How to Zing! Your Life and Leadership* was written to eliminate the various compartments of your life or leadership (i.e. office worker, family member, industry leader, parent, boss, daughter, son, manager, student leader, volunteer, etc.) and replace them with one whole—

or complete—human being. To achieve this goal, I combined my own insights with strategies, laws, habits, principles, and tips from today's more popular motivational and leadership thinkers. The result is twenty-one insights towards a more meaningful life and influential style of leadership.

WHY DO I NEED ZING!?

You hold in your hand yet another self-help-instructional-how-to book. This one, however, is neither solely about life nor solely about leadership. It's about *Zing!*—that thing which happens when you combine your life with your leadership to produce a higher quality product, improve your relationships, and serve a greater good. Despite the "humility is in—charisma is out" tune sung by those feeling the sting of the "it's all about me" charismatic leader, this book *is* about charisma. It is about becoming better, wiser, smarter, and more influential—all for the benefit of making the world a better place because *you* showed up!

HOW ZING! WORKS

If you are a by-product of the self-actualized-self-helped-self-managed generation of the 1980s, you might rejuvenate your *Zing!* potential simply by reading the Table of Contents. However, if you want to know why you need to embark on this journey of self-discovery and make the needed self-improvements, then read each of the twenty-one insights. The first insight appropriately begins with the topic of self-inspection, and the last keeps your feet on the ground with a discussion about humility. Each insight contains an opportunity for assessment (found in Appendix A: Chapter Self-Assessments) and a skill building lesson. The more frequently you practice each lesson, the more it will become part of your personality, and the more influential you will become. As a result of reading this book, you will have the tools you need to accomplish your goals on a daily basis and discover a renewed sense of happiness as you use your time and talents to make this world a better place.

So, do you want happiness?

Is *Zing!* in your future?

1

GETTING WHAT YOU WANT

"Nothing ever great was achieved without enthusiasm."
—Ralph Waldo Emerson

When all is said and done, only one thing really matters in this world. Some call it the "secret of life." Some call it "the secret of success." Some call it the "gift of prophecy" or "visionary thinking." I don't think it's a secret at all. In fact, I don't think it's all that difficult to discover what really matters—that "one thing" that answers all the questions you have ever asked about the meaning of life, the definition of success, or the essence of true leadership. The one thing we all seek in this world is happiness.

Are you happy? I mean really happy?

Do you have what you want in your life or are you settling for whatever comes your way?

Are you handling what you've received in life—the good, bad, and ugly—with grace or despair?

Is the world a better place because you get out of bed every morning?

If being happy matters to you (and it should), then it's time for you to delete those attitudes and behaviors holding you back and release the *Zing!* (exclamation point required) from within. *Zing!* is a good thing. *Zing!* is a means to a happier end, the path to a successful life. It's what will get you to where you are going, but it's not the destination—it's the journey.

DEFINING SUCCESS

Definitions of "having it all," "happiness," or "success," when written by anyone other than the person living that particular life, are

1

unproductive and impersonal. I once tried to reach for those other defined standards as a full-time mother of two infants, full-time wife, full-time housekeeper, full- time professional, full-time community member, and full-time daughter. But all I became was a full- time nutcase. I wasn't making a difference; I was making a living. No. *You* have to define for yourself where you want to go; *Zing!* will help get you there.

SUCCESSFUL WANTING

WHAT DO YOU WANT?

Are you looking for the corner office, a promotion, or the opportunity to present your own reports at staff meetings? Would you find happiness in going from a B student to an A student? Do you want to be followed into the restroom by no less than six colleagues, become the president of a large corporation, or start your own business? Maybe you want to change the world one child at a time. Whether or not you realize it, you want something. Consider if your actions are trying to tell you it's time to put your needs first. The last time you were in a bookstore, was there a reason your feet kept taking you directly to the books on saving your marriage, 101 ways to be a better parent, or how to get a date?

Many people know what they want; they just don't feel worthy of happiness. Believe that you deserve more. Know that you are on this planet for a reason. Your life has purpose—even if you haven't figured out what that is yet. Go for what you want. Follow your heart. Write your own story. Your destiny is the paper; *Zing!* is the pen.

Thought by thought, you control your destiny by making choices about how you spend your time and where you exert your influence. From seconds to minutes, from minutes to hours, and from hours to days, your attitude, behaviors, and purpose combine to create you at any moment—happy or sad. Your choices impact—and change— other people. You create the energy that attracts or repulses others to or from your causes, efforts, and personality. This energy is your personal magnetism, ability to influence, or charisma. It's the *it* you wish you had when you needed *it*, the silent and not-so-silent force that accompanies you into a room with noticeable confidence.

THE DEFINITION OF CHARISMA

Charisma is *Zing!*. It applies not only to your leadership, but also to your life. Charisma is often hard to describe because it is so personal in nature, and until recently, considered too subjective to measure. Leadership through a less self-serving model of charisma is a growing phenomenon.

THE RELATIONAL NATURE OF CHARISMA

Harvard University anthropologist Charles Lindholm, as quoted in *Charisma* by Dr. Tony Alessandra, states: "charisma can be revealed only in interaction with others." It's a function of how others view you, not how you view yourself. Charismatic leaders need followers. Therefore, your charismatic potential (or *Zing!*) is determined by the reverence (or lack of) others have for you based upon your interactions with them.

If a tree falls in the forest and no one hears it, does it make a sound? If you crack yourself up laughing while alone in your room, are you really all that funny? Likewise, if you consider yourself to be a charismatic leader, or hold a position of leadership that includes your name on the door but (and it's a big "but") no one follows you, are you all that influential? No.

Charisma involves connecting to others on a variety of levels, including intellectual, emotional, spiritual, and physical. It is a multi-dimensional construct requiring another force (or forces) to be present so that a stronger influence can be exerted against that particular force. Charisma is a valuable skill and a powerful means of influencing others, achieving personal happiness, and making the world a better place. However, for this to be the case, a more clearly articulated purpose—or utilization—needs to be added to the definition, such as "positively influencing others towards a greater social good."

This book offers another perspective to a phenomenon that has intrigued humans for centuries and continually changes in meaning. In fact, organizational behaviorist Rakesh Khurana suggests that since its adaptation from Christian theology, charisma has evolved to mean a "set of personal qualities that inspire awe and submission in others." After considerable study, he concludes: "charisma remains as difficult to define as art or love. Few who advocate it are able to convey what they mean by the term."[1] I believe the term will continue to evolve as the world's needs for charismatic leadership evolves.

THE ORIGIN OF CHARISMA

The word *charisma* is derived from the Greek translation "gift of favor or tongue." *Charms* is the root—a Greek word meaning "favor." The suffix *ma* (meaning "gift of") was added later. The first use of the term traces back to Christianity. The apostle Paul uses *charms* in the New Testament when speaking of church leaders and other disciples who possess the "gifts of the Holy Spirit." As noted by Khurana: "according to Paul, those gifted with charisma included 'good leaders'. . . [and] church members with extraordinary endowments, such as the power to speak in tongues or work miracles."[2] This connotation is commonly assumed when someone asks, "Who would you identify as a charismatic leader?" I often hear the names of great orators like Elizabeth Dole, Dr. Martin Luther King Jr., and Winston Churchill, for example. I also hear the names of great corporate icons, like Jack Welch of General Electric, Carly Fiorina of Hewlett-Packard, David Stern of the National Basketball Association, and Oprah Winfrey of Harpo Productions. These are the "superstars." They influence others to do great things.

THE CEO CORPORATE SUPERSTARS

One of the first leaders to fit the "CEO Superstar" definition of charisma was Lee Iaccoca, former chairman of the Chrysler Corporation. Unlike many of his modern counterparts, he moved up through the ranks of the same company he eventually headed. Today, many "charismatic superstars" are transplanted from other organizations, never having paid their dues in the dynasty they now control.

Although a shift is taking place, a degree of celebrity is still associated with and expected from a majority of today's high-powered, high-profile corporate leaders. It's not uncommon to see their faces on the cover of *Newsweek*, *The Wall Street Journal*, and *People*. Earning million-dollar salaries, flying in corporate jets, and moving from one empire to another, these types of superstars serve to shape, salvage, and often reinvent their respective corporation's image almost single-handedly (at least that's what they'd like their stockholders to believe).

THE CHANGING MEANING OF CHARISMA

The nature and meaning of charisma has changed over time for a variety of reasons. First and foremost, the negative backlash of corporate scandals involving flashy CEO corporate superstars makes it necessary to question in this day and age whether it's good or bad to be a "charismatic leader." Secondly, most Americans are discovering that despite corporate leaders' high levels of competency, we cannot realistically assume that one person can make or break an entire corporation. This assumption ignores the significant role of domestic and global forces—especially terrorist attacks, stock market drops, and war. Rudolph Guiliani, for example, wasn't viewed as a charismatic leader until after September 11, 2001. Previously, he had to overcome bad publicity from a very public divorce and was known for his "tough" style of leadership, especially regarding crime and law enforcement.

A PERSONAL CHALLENGE

This book was written to encourage you to go beyond a narrow application of charisma and inspire you to consider the role of *influence* or *enhanced "charizma"* in your every day life and leadership. Look around at the people with whom you interact on a daily basis. There you will find examples of great people doing great things: teachers, neighbors, community volunteers, coaches, teenagers, and storeowners living their lives and leadership with *Zing!*.

THE PERSONALITY OF INFLUENCE

What does it take to be more influential and charismatic? Researchers Jay A. Conger, Rabindra N. Kanungo, and Sanjay T. Menon have added new understanding to what I call "the personality of influence." Their work builds upon existing behavioral dimensions of charismatic leadership to encourage more empirical studies. In addition, they have successfully identified specific "follower effects" of charismatic leaders to include follower's reverence, sense of group identity, and perceived group task performance with charismatic leadership.[3] Now you can assess if you have the same traits as those individuals considered by others to be effective leaders.

MEASURING CHARISMA

One such measurement tool developed by Conger and Kanungo is a 20-item, psychometrically sound measure of assessing charismatic leadership called the "Conger-Kanungo Charismatic Leadership Scale."[4] The scale features five significant variables of charismatic leadership, including: strategic vision and articulation, personal risk, sensitivity to the environment, sensitivity to member's needs, and unconventional behavior. These variables were consistent with many other sources identifying leadership traits by followers (which will be discussed in later chapters).

I have developed the "Personality of Influence Inventory" as a measure of your ability to influence or *Zing!*. This is your first assessment opportunity (or pre-test). To measure your improvement, I have also included this inventory as your last opportunity for self-assessment (or post-test). The Inventory lists sixty traits—or "small things"—that contribute to your ability to *Zing!*. Take a moment right now to go to Appendix A: Chapter Self-Assessments and evaluate your current level of *Zing!*.

PUTTING ALL THE PIECES TOGETHER

The more consistently you make each of the traits listed in the Inventory part of your personality, the greater your potential to be more influential and charismatic, and the greater chance for others to notice you as such. Understanding how all of these traits come together, combined with external forces, will allow you to use what you've got when you need it! The *Zing!* Impact Equation (introduced in the next chapter) illustrates the complexity of maximizing your influence.

"You make a living by what you get.
You make a life by what you give."
—Winston Churchill

2

FORMULA FOR SUCCESS

"When people are serving, life is no longer meaningless."
—*John W. Gardner*

I must admit: I never wanted to be a brain surgeon, airline pilot, firefighter, second grade substitute teacher, or secret agent. Not because I wasn't willing to work that hard, but rather because none of it was something I wanted to do—way too scary. Bungee jumping, riding the Tower of Terror at MGM Studios, or skydiving aren't on my "to do" list either. My chosen method of adventure is neither a profession nor a thrill ride; it's movies. *Jaws*. To this day, a low-thumping sound of "dah-dah" sends me jumping on a chair.

What do you know about you? To answer this question requires considerable honesty. What brings you joy? What gives your life a sense of purpose? Life itself is a job. You get up, get dressed, and "go to work." Your attendance is required and at the end you have a performance review. Life is the best kind of occupation because you are self-employed. You're the boss. Regardless of what you may think, you get to choose what contribution or difference you will make in this world. You get to define your own success.

TRUTH

The ability to do what you want to do is the purest form of truth. If you aren't searching for truth, then you aren't seeking happiness. If happiness really isn't important to you, if you'd rather play the martyr, stay miserable, live a beige existence, waste your talents, and make the people around you miserable, then stop reading this book. You will never have *Zing!* if you lead a hypocritical life. You will never have followers if people doubt the sincerity of your direction or question your motives. Your leadership isn't possible without your life. The desire to reach your fullest potential, in both your life and leadership, matters. When you have achieved this sense of applied integrity, you have achieved truth.

FORMULA FOR MAXIMIZING YOUR INFLUENCE

How to *Zing!* your life and leadership is demonstrated in the *Zing!* Impact Equation. The goal of this equation is to simplify a rather complex process by illustrating four significant components that affect people's receptivity of your life and leadership. As previously noted, charisma is a function of how others see and receive you. Your charismatic potential at any given moment is determined by the degree of reverence you inspire in others at that moment. You need to look at the entire picture—or contextual framework—of the experience of your presence from another's point of view. To simply focus on one trait of charisma (i.e. giving a great speech) without taking into account the environment in which you are giving it (i.e. audience characteristics, current events, physical set-up of venue, etc.) is to lower the bar on your charismatic potential.

ZING! IMPACT EQUATION

The formula below illustrates how your charismatic potential, hereby referred to as *Zing!* Quotient (ZQ) is a function of *internally* controlled forces such as your personality, appearance, and style of communication, in combination with *externally* controlled environmental factors, use of twenty-one insights, and the negative consequences of distracting behaviors (individual detractors).

Your charismatic potential (Zing! Quotient) = f(person) + environment + insights – individual detractors
Zing! Quotient (ZQ) = f(P) + E + I - ID

This equation takes into account how "competing forces" can be personal, such as physical disability, language barrier, race or illness. Or, they can be part of your every day environment, such as the people you work with, classmates, or the nature of what you do for a living. The factors of the *Zing!* Impact Equation show you how to use the areas you control to compensate for those areas controlled by forces greater than you. Your ability to influence is not only a function of your individual traits, but also your individual traits as they interact with the environment. As a result, both of these are impacted by your ability to understand and apply the twenty-one insights or eliminate traits of significant distraction.

Using this formula, you can see how any person, including you, can be charismatic or influential at *any* given time. In addition, it's easy to see how the entire equation can be significantly affected by just one part of the equation. Each component of the equation is reviewed in more detail below.

PERSON (P)

Your ability to positively influence others begins with you: the person. Consider the reality, "wherever you go, there you are." For example, if you have poor relationships, don't excel at your place of employment, are continually passed over for leadership positions, and lack a network of support, the one consistent element in all of these situations is you. That's right, you! It is totally possible that you lack *Zing!*—that thing that you bring to your everything! This doesn't mean you can't get *Zing!*, but the more you know about the traits of charisma, for example, the greater the odds you will be able to identify your starting point of self-improvement.

The (P) part of the *Zing!* Impact Equation includes all aspects of your being: who you take with you wherever you go. The good and the bad. The charismatic and the unimpressive. The "person" part of the equation is literally what others see and feel in your presence. This is you, as you have chosen to present yourself. Included within this category are the following:

- Personality
- Disposition
- Appearance
- Attitude
- Style of communication
- The frequency of your smile
- How you greet and meet others
- The care you take in your appearance
- Physical conditioning

- Health and wellness practices
- The way you process information (right or left brained?)
- Intelligence
- Sense of humor
- Comfort level of risk
- Interests and hobbies
- Practicing faith
- What life gives you
    (i.e. death of a spouse, illness, birth of a child)
- Response to crisis
- Support group
- Position in a family
- Social circle
- Beliefs and philosophy of life

Many of these characteristics are under your control, whether you believe it or not. Take your appearance, for example. You can always find a way to look more appealing. I'm not advocating "extreme makeovers" and I don't believe people should be judged according to what's on the outside. However, how you present yourself *does* matter if your goal is to positively influence others. From pressing your clothes to wearing the appropriate attire, you will learn how small adjustments can make a big difference. Good, bad, or indifferent, a heightened sense of awareness to what others literally see when they look at you affects the person (P) part of your ZQ.

ENVIRONMENT (E)

The second influential component of the *Zing!* Impact Equation is the *environment* or conditions under which others interact with you. Presence is the first condition. Place, time, culture, role, and physical location also make up the environment part of your equation. The following list represents a sample of (E) factors in your *Zing!* Quotient:

- Where you work
- What classes you attend
- The weather
- Stress from external forces

- Common meeting ground or place
- The medium carrying your message
- What's going on in the world
- Others' expectations of you
- Home life
- Organization or community involvement

You don't always need to be physically present to be present to others. Someone who thinks about you, maybe even makes the comment, "I wish (your name) could see this!" is illustrating the significance of presence. In addition, coaching a little league team, helping someone cross the street, hugging a crying child, complimenting your secretary, or sending flowers to someone are all ways to be present in someone else's environment. When a child says, "I shouldn't do this; my coach wouldn't like it" illustrates how the presence of the relationship influences the child's decision-making.

THE HUMAN AGGREGATE

Another kind of presence or environment is the "human aggregate." This environment is created when a collection of individuals come together. The environment of a room filled with college students, for instance, is different when that same room is filled with sixth-graders. "Mandatory" audiences, for example, create a different learning environment than those who come of their own free will. The environment of a room filled with your relatives, for example, is different from a room filled with strangers. Expand your awareness of your environment and you will expand your ZQ.

To assist you in understanding the significant role of environment (E) in your *Zing!* Impact Equation, I've compared the manner in which Princess Diana and Mother Teresa used the media.

A PRINCESS AND A SAINT

Mother Teresa (1910 – 1997) liked to stay out of the public's attention, quietly going about her work. She neither sought the limelight nor used the media to advance her causes. Her approach was to lead by example and be the caregiver. In contrast, Princess Diana (1961 – 1997) was masterful at bringing media attention to her causes (i.e.

AIDS awareness, land mine removal, etc.) and effectively used her environment as a means to advance her causes. This difference in approaches was most evident upon their deaths, only five days apart. Princess Diana's death was a mega-media event. Mother Teresa died quietly in her Missionaries of Charity home in central Calcutta. Her death, albeit covered by national news media, was simply overshadowed by Diana's coverage. Despite the significant contributions both women made to society, as well as the profound lessons they taught others on a daily basis, the way they achieved what they achieved differed vastly.

TWENTY-ONE INSIGHTS ON LIFE AND LEADERSHIP (I)

The third component of the *Zing!* Impact Equation is based on the belief that the right combination of small things can have a big impact. I recently asked a professional recruiter about the most sought-after characteristics of her top candidates. Her response supported my multi-faceted approach to charisma building: "A host of things—not just one. It's never just one thing." She observes candidates from the time they arrive to the interview to how they treat the wait-staff during lunch. She also spoke about the importance of integrity and how she evaluates this trait in a very short time with a candidate. Her observations of the smaller things lead her to big conclusions and important decisions.

MORE IS BETTER!

When you buy into a majority of the insights offered on the following pages for the majority of the time, you will achieve a greater *Zing!* Quotient than if you only adopt a few once in a while. In this case, more is better! You can go from *wanting* to *achieving*, and from *observing* to *doing*, if you truly maximize your effort to learn about and use all twenty-one insights (and their accompanying skill building lessons.) Although you will have to consciously think about and practice some of the new and improved behaviors for each insight, do so knowing that each behavior supports a particular insight. Eventually, you will use the right skill or attitude at just the right time. This ability differentiates those who "get it" from those who don't. The twenty-one insights (I) include the following:

The ability to self-examine
A congruent content of character
A clearly defined purpose
A clearly articulated vision for the future
Courage
The ability to transcend adversity
Adaptability
A positive attitude
The habit of praising others
The ability to show respect
The ability to nourish your mind, heart and soul
Intelligence (or love of learning)
Determination
The ability to actively listen
Interpersonal communication skills
The pursuit of public speaking opportunities
The ability to maintain and create healthy relationships
A fun sense of humor
Playfulness
Self-discipline
Humility

INDIVIDUAL DETRACTORS (ID)

The final component of the *Zing!* Impact Equation, *individual detractors* (ID), is a behavior or set of behaviors representing an attitude or belief *not* viewed favorably by most people. Individual detractors are negatives. They take away from your *Zing!* Quotient and are often what people remember most about you (hence, your true ID). You want to eliminate whatever is subtracting from your ability to positively influence others so as to maximize your ZQ. You can have all twenty-one insights down, be at the right place and at the right time, and nail your presentation; but if you yawn without covering your mouth—which projects apparent boredom with everything and everyone around you—and that small, yet significant, action is noticed by all, the latter has far outweighed the former. You blew it.

LESS IS SOMETIMES MORE

I'm amazed at how much attention people give to the "big stuff" and how they don't do the "easy stuff." Based upon my theory, both kinds of "stuff" have the same potential to either raise or lower your ZQ. Using the above example, why would you spend hours preparing a presentation, for instance, and then forget to cover your mouth when you yawn in public? Are you suggesting that the people around you need to be excited in your presence, but you don't need to be excited in their presence? Knowing instinctively which skill set or behaviors not to employ at any given time can be as valuable as knowing all twenty-one insights.

Don't make the mistake of thinking the following list of individual detractors isn't a negative for someone somewhere. Every item below consistently appeared on surveys in which participants were asked to list "non-charismatic" behaviors or "things that bug you about people." Whether or not you agree with some of the items isn't the point. Remember, charisma is about how others receive you!

- Over-exaggerates own accomplishments
- Finds faults, not remedies
- Speaks negatively about others, or gossips
- Tells racist or sexist jokes
- Chews gum loudly
- Wears noticeably non-pressed clothes
- Takes unearned credit for work
- Uses words like "whatever"
- Arrives late to appointments
- Acts out of ego
- Forgets people's names
- Doesn't smile when passing someone
- Fails to maintain eye contact
- Takes shoes off in others' presence
- Clicks the end of pen in a distracting manner
- Does not consider others' feelings
- Doesn't hold a door open for others
- Cuts ahead of others in line
- Hasn't read a book for pleasure in a month

- Monopolizes conversations or doesn't engage in conversations
- Appears disorganized or discombobulated
- Tells inappropriate jokes
- Stays too long (or not long enough) at social functions
- Looks at his or her watch during a conversation
- Smokes without asking if others mind
- Cares little about others' welfare
- Has poor dinner etiquette
- Boasts about being "bored"
- Brags about being "dumb"
- Speaks with food in his or her mouth
- Yells at others
- Cannot be trusted with a confidence
- Cheats or is less than honest
- Can't say "I'm sorry" when wrong
- Doesn't return phone calls

How Low Can We Go Club

Just when I think I've seen it all, I get on yet another plane! On a flight into Washington, D.C., a well-dressed man took his seat in the First Class cabin. I sat directly behind him. Using my exceptional detective skills, I pegged him as a regional vice-president for some company (I saw his luggage tag).

Shortly before take off, I noticed that this hadn't been a good day for him. I also noticed that he was going to make sure it wasn't a good day for anyone else. Maybe it was the manner in which he literally chucked a bag of pretzels back at the flight attendant because "he expected more out of First Class" or the fact he took off his shoes, leaving his stinky feet for the rest of us to smell, which demonstrated his self-serving approach to life. He might have looked like a million bucks, but I wouldn't give two cents for his opinion about anything.

But he was in good company. Although I wasn't invited to join, other passengers on this flight started their own "How Low Can We Go?" club. The woman seated behind me discussed her divorce loudly on her cell phone. For the rest of us (including the pretzel-chucking, foot-smelling VP), this meant acting as if we couldn't hear what should have been a very personal and private conversation. When the woman sitting to her left (apparently not invited to join the club either) commented that it sounded like she was going through a tough time, the newest member of the club's ZQ plummeted with a sharp, "Why don't you mind your own business!"

Important Note: Poor cell phone etiquette is an individual detractor. You should talk out of others' earshot, not because *you* want privacy; but rather because *other* people shouldn't have to hear your conversation!

Shoe's on the Other Foot

One of the ways to determine the behaviors and characteristics that subtract from your ZQ is to identify in others what you find repulsive, obnoxious, distasteful, immature, disgusting, boring, unappealing…well, you get the idea. Take a moment and ask yourself, "Who is the most unappealing person I know?" Hopefully, you are not the answer. Consider what specifically causes you to think this way. This verifies the belief that small things can have a large impact on others' perceptions of you.

The Payoffs of Maximizing Your Zing! Potential

Being more influential and being able to attract others' reverence can net positive results, not only for your life and leadership, but also for those around you. Consider how increasing your ability to override competing forces to positively influence others can also help you to do the following:

- Take good relationships and make them great
- Create opportunities for others to be taught
- Enrich others' lives through your presence
- Accomplish your organization's goals more efficiently
- Recruit more involvement
- Inspire others to work towards your goals

- Establish and build new relationships
- Serve as a role model or mentor to inspire others
- Give others perspective
- Make a difference

ZING! MOMENTUM

As you review the many insights offered on the following pages, your friends, family, colleagues, associates, and neighbors, for instance, will almost immediately interact with you differently. You will then respond to them differently. As this charismatic momentum builds, you will experience a satisfying sense of accomplishment. A word of caution, however: others may not always appreciate your efforts for self-improvement, especially if they are accustomed to interacting with the more self-focused you. They may become confused or question your motives. If you consistently apply your new insights, in time they will trust you. Begin now by paying more attention to how people respond to you. Specifically, ask yourself, "What raises or lowers my Zing! Quotient?" Self-improvement always begins with honest self-assessment.

"Habits change into character."
— Ovid

LIFE AND LEADERSHIP

"Life is too short to be little."
—Benjamin Disraeli

I'm short. I'm always going to be short. In fact, I'll probably only get shorter. I can't change this fact of nature. I can, however, request a wireless microphone before I speak so I don't have to stand behind a podium and look like a talking nose. I can stay fit so I stand vertically, not horizontally. After being introduced to them at social functions, I can ask tall people to sit so that my neck doesn't break during a fifteen-minute conversation. I have learned how to work with what I've got so I can get what I want—that is, to make a difference! I've also learned that life and leadership go hand and hand; you don't get one without the other.

When I was younger, I couldn't understand what people meant by the term "hand in hand"—what a strange thing to say. I continued to build upon this erroneous grammatical structure believing I was correct—or more accurately, not believing I was wrong. During graduate school, my error in usage was quickly brought to my attention, prompting me to quickly replace my term for "hand and hand." This experience taught me something very valuable. Practice *doesn't* make perfect if you are practicing incorrectly. Perfect practice makes perfect.

MAKING THE CONNECTION

You have a life. Are you living it right? You are a leader. Do you have followers? Consider the reality that you have 100% of expendable energy every morning when you get out of bed. Life and leadership requires all of your energy, not just a percentage. You are one person with one heart, one intellect, one spirit, and more. All of your thoughts belong to you. All of your skills are yours. Decisions about your life are also decisions about your leadership. To be successful, treat your ability to live with as much passion as you treat your ability to influence others, and vice versa. You are here to enhance not only your immediate surrounding but also society as a whole. I've never met anyone who dedicates his or her life to making others' lives better and is totally unhappy.

Characteristics of leadership need to be applied consistently across all aspects of your life. Being an effective mediator at work, for example, should imply you are also an effective mediator at home. If I observe you yelling at your child in the grocery store, then I'm not likely to walk into your office for counsel because I'm having trouble with a subordinate. Likewise, you can't expect me to confide in you as a friend after you've just shared extremely personal information about a mutual acquaintance. Nothing is more disturbing than meeting career counselors who hate their jobs, healthcare professionals who smoke, or receiving notes home from your child's teacher containing spelling errors. Consistency in your behaviors matters.

LEADERSHIP DEFINED

Leadership is the ability to make a difference. It is not a professional or personal wardrobe. You don't put it on in the morning, like a tie, and take it off at night. Leadership is how things change. One of America's greatest leadership scholars, John W. Gardner, offers: "Leadership is the process of persuasion or example by which an individual (or leadership team) induces a group to pursue objectives held by the leader or shared by the leader and his or her followers." In other words, your goal as leader is to inspire others to action. Another great leadership educator John C. Maxwell, confirms: "Leadership is influence—nothing more, nothing less." *Zing!* is a process or means of carrying out your leadership.

THE TITLE MISTAKE

Leadership is not about the position; it's about the person. You can have the titles, a corner office, and diplomas on your walls, but if you aren't a decent human being concerned about making a positive contribution in the world, you aren't a leader. Positions and titles are often the very things that can prevent you from doing what truly matters. They can restrict your freedom to be creative, require that you spend valuable time and resources fighting off negative influences, and hold you contractually to carrying out someone else's mission as opposed to your own. Just because you are in the "position" of head delegate, representative, president, manager, teacher, or student doesn't necessarily make it truth in the eyes of others. Your goal is to live and lead with applied integrity.

MISTAKEN IDENTITY

My son Jake and I went to Washington, D.C. for his tenth birthday. While boarding the plane, I reminded him of proper plane etiquette. Apparently, I had made my point relatively early in our conversation, because as I began to open my mouth on our way down the jet way, he commented, "I get it already." Enjoying the frequent flyer perks, we were the first to board the plane and find our seats in First Class. Jake's backpack was rather well-stuffed and he was having difficulty storing it in the overhead bin.

As he struggled, other First Class passengers boarded and quickly became frustrated at having to wait while my son fiddled with his backpack. Waiting to take their seats did not prevent them, however, from commenting to the parties on their cell phones about the delay Jake was causing them. Within earshot one man said, "I'll be in my seat as soon as this little kid gets his act together... he should be in coach, anyway." Jake quickly pulled down his backpack and stepped away from the aisle. At this point, and as though their rudeness had earned them the right, they completely stuffed the exact bin my son was attempting to use with their own luggage!

We were dumbfounded. Together, we stuffed his bag under the seat in front of us, leaving him with no leg room. I leaned over and said quietly, "Hey, Birthday Boy, always remember this: just because you sit in First Class, doesn't mean you are first class." (I resisted the temptation to say it louder.)

INTENTIONS MATTER

Leadership, just like your life, is a 24-7-365 proposition. Either you are in or you are out! All or nothing! The decision to make a difference is really a decision to use your talents and time to do good. Technically, Hitler was a phenomenal leader—if you define a leader as someone who can influence others to do whatever he or she wants them to do. Making a difference is making the *right* difference. Your motives matter. Good intentions live behind the actions of influential leaders. You live your life to help others and make a positive contribution. Whether building houses for senior citizens, planning mission trips for your youth group, owning a general store, or being a director of admissions at a school for learning disabled children; when your efforts result in a greater good, you make a difference. You are a leader.

MATTER OVER MONEY

The majority of educators I am blessed to know teach because they want their students to learn. It's not about the money; it's about making a difference. Conversely, just because someone makes a lot of money doesn't mean they aren't capable of serving a greater good. Just because they devote their time and talents to building a corporation doesn't mean they aren't concerned or committed to making the world a better place. Just because someone sits in the front of the plane doesn't mean they will take their shoes off or be insulting to your child. Senior researcher at Yale Law School, former president of Connecticut College, and author of *The Greater Good* Claire Gaudiani states: "It's not that Americans have been generous because we're rich, we're rich because we have been generous." Her research confirms both the visible and invisible impact of philanthropy in America.[1] My rule: *It doesn't matter how much money you make; it matters what you do with the money you've got!*

Whether you flip burgers at McDonalds, head a major university, or drive the shuttle bus around the airport parking lot, you have an opportunity to influence others' lives in a positive way. If you don't believe, however, that your leadership counts—or worse yet, that you aren't a leader—then why should I? Why would I be a better person for having interacted with you, if you don't think you have the ability to make me a better person? Being a leader begins by believing you are a leader.

LIFE DEFINED

Consider the following definitions of "life." Betty Talmadge said: "Life is what you get when you're making other plans," and W. C. Handy said: "*Life* is like a trumpet: if you don't put anything in, you won't get anything out." In my first book *Life by Design: A Do-It-Yourself Approach to Achieving Happiness*, I defined life according to how we spend our time. In other words, define life as you live your life. Communicate your priorities by the manner in which you spend your time.

If you say you want more *Zing!*, the question becomes: *What are you willing to change in your life to make this happen?* What are you willing to give up, add on, adjust, and/or tweak? You have twenty-four hours in a day. (Despite our desire for thirty-six, the hours in a day are fixed.) That's why time becomes one of the most significant competing forces to overcome when working towards increasing your ZQ. You must, however, figure out a way to embrace change and do things differently if you are going to maximize the standards of your life and leadership.

CHARACTERISTICS OF INFLUENTIAL LEADERS

Because *charisma*, by its very definition, is a feeling of reverence or an inspired desire to follow someone towards a greater social good, it is helpful to examine who and what inspires you. Who do you admire and why? What qualifies someone to be a "role model" in your eyes, while someone else is passed by? You answer these questions by using your value system because charisma is in the eye of the beholder. Likewise, it doesn't matter what you (or I) *think* people want from your life and leadership; it matters what *they* want. Within the twenty-one insights offered on the following pages are "best guesses" of what others want from your life and leadership; experience will be your ultimate teacher.

ADMIRABLE CHARACTERISTICS

Charismatic or influential leaders are also individuals who, in many cases, have overcome the tragedies, hardships, and challenges life has given them with a huge amount of grace. They do not complain. They never notice what they lack and others appear to possess. They don't ask, "Why me?" They use their life experience to help others get through their struggles with less pain. Their generosity flows freely. In addition, influential people who inspire admiration possess a powerful faith, a belief in treating people equally, and strong commitment to keeping their lives simple. Family is a priority. Not only do they donate their time and talents, they give of their resources.

Neighbors, co-workers, colleagues, children, and members of your tennis club, will follow you if you work hard, listen attentively, and put their needs ahead of your own. If you take care of yourself, practice what you preach, and are extremely honest, you'll impact them. Leaders follow their hearts, accomplish remarkable things, and aren't afraid to learn new things or take chances. One of most admirable traits of leaders with *Zing!* is their desire to make time for others, make them feel safe, and encourage them to achieve their dreams. They are supportive, not competitive. Leaders with *Zing!* are hopeful about the future, bring joy and laughter to the world, and give money to various causes. They count their blessings and their friends, say "Hello" to strangers, and treat others with kindness. In short, you will admire them for those traits you wish you possessed.

LIVING FOR OTHERS

Consider how these characteristics fit the individuals described below. These individuals all have something in common: they are or were charismatic and influential leaders. They dedicated (or are dedicating) their lives to making a difference in others' lives. Despite completely different means of impact, or "environments of influence," these individuals served, and continue to serve humanity with their gifts and talents. They possess the *Zing!* I'm encouraging you to possess. Using faith, humor, and compassion, for example, they made (and make) the world a better place because of their unique abilities to override competing forces to positively impact others.

MOTHER TERESA:

When most people were afraid for their own health, Mother Teresa lived among the sick, poor and dying in Calcutta bringing comfort and care. Her life was devoted to giving hope to the hopeless in more than one hundred and twenty countries. She inspired a world to "translate our spiritual beliefs into action in the world."[2]

BOB HOPE:

Despite the dangers of war, Bob Hope spent much of World War II traveling the world to entertain Allied troops. He brought laughter to the troops in Korea, Vietnam, and the Middle East. He continued to entertain troops up to the late 1990s. His legacy continues to inspire entertainers to give of their time and talents for those willing to give their lives for our freedom.

MIA HAMM:

Understatedly one of the most prominent female sports figures of our time, Mia Hamm has never sought the spotlight for herself, but rather for her sport, country, and teammates. Her goal is to advance women's soccer, not her own celebrity.

JIMMY CARTER:

Former president, Noble Peace prizewinner, and author, Jimmy Carter is often the first to pick up a hammer and work alongside of heat-drenched volunteers building homes for the less fortunate in support of Habit for Humanity. Through his writings, Christian faith and humanitarian programs of The Carter Center, Jimmy Carter continues to influence nations.[3]

MILLARD FULLER:

As founder and president of Habitat for Humanity International (founded in 1976), Millard Fuller advocates decent and affordable housing for all. He is the recipient of the Presidential Medal of Freedom. His efforts have transformed thousands of lives and made the dream of home ownership a reality.

FRED ROGERS:

An ordained minister, accomplished musician, and composer, Mr. Rogers began one of the first publicly broadcasted television programs on PBS (*Mister Roger's Neighborhood*) dedicated to teaching values and a sense of belonging to children.

CONNECTING WITH CHARISMA

In all of the above examples, you recognize that no blatant separation (or compartmentalization) exists between life and leadership; they are one and the same. Throughout the chapters to follow, you will read about individuals whose names you might not recognize because they aren't famous—but, they are exceptionable human beings whose lives and leadership have inspired and positively influenced so many. Their stories demonstrate how every human being can achieve happiness despite significant obstacles and make the world a better place.

TIMING IS EVERYTHING

How will you know it's your turn to be the leader? When do you go from beige to colorful? The difficult part of making a difference is timing. People are perceptive. They can tell almost instinctively whether you are being inconvenienced or committed to helping people when they need your help. Leadership rarely happens when you hold a meeting, rally, or organizational event. Leadership happens when someone is *in need* of direction and influence. This means it happens on *their* time, not always on *your* time. It is often difficult to know whether you made the impact or difference you wanted to make. In addition, you don't always get the benefit of more than one contact or chance to make a difference. It's important to believe—from the inside out—that your life and leadership matters all the time (24–7–365). You have a life. You are a leader. It's *Zing!* time.

*"Keep away from people who try to belittle your ambitions.
Small people always do that, but the really great make you feel that
you, too, can become great."*
—Mark Twain

4

ZING! TIME

"Success is the maximum utilization of the ability you have."
—Zig Ziglar

Have you ever been a chaperone? It's an adventure. I think chaperones need other chaperones. On a four-day camping trip with my son's fourth grade class, I learned two things: parents should not be left unattended, and children can be taught to take only what they can eat. Really! You can teach children (and adults) how to decrease wasted food. The key is to weigh the amount of leftover food at each table following every meal. As tables compete to have the lowest number, the total amount of wasted food in the room goes down. (Of course, at camp a song accompanies the ritual of weighing the leftover food, but I've conveniently forgotten it.) The success of reducing wasteful eating behaviors is a direct result of each consumer knowing in advance the role he or she plays in the total score. Aside from parents hiding unused apples down their shirts, the children made a remarkable discovery in four short days. They learned an important lesson about world hunger while being fed. They learned how one person makes a difference. All they needed for this lesson was a set of rules (or perspective), a scale, and a song. They achieved a greater social good because a counselor took the time to "set the stage." Now, the table is set for your field trip...

THE PRINCIPLES OF ZING!

Before you *Zing!* I'm giving you four significant principles that will assist you in your search for a more charismatic and influential you. By accepting these principles, you remove the pressure of

comparison to others' leadership abilities and increase the usefulness of the information presented throughout this book.

PRINCIPLE ONE: YOU DO GET A SECOND CHANCE
TO MAKE A GOOD FIRST IMPRESSION.

This principle acknowledges the fact you are human. You will
screw up. You will walk out of a bathroom with toilet paper stuck to
the bottom of your shoe. Buttons will pop. Zippers will unzip.
Because you are tired, words you've just invented will spill out of your
mouth, you'll say things you don't mean, and neglect to say things
you should. More often than not, you have time to fix what you
momentarily break, apologize, or make it right. I caution you against
writing someone or something off prematurely (including you).

PRINCIPLE TWO: LET IT GO!

If the damage is too great to repair, remember this second principle and LET IT GO! It's over. You can't turn back time or erase
a memory in someone else's mind. Think of your high school days
or your first day on a college campus. Remember walking into the
wrong class and staying there for the entire duration of class because
you didn't want anyone else to know you were a freshman? For those
of us who have tripped going *up* stairs, we share the bond of knowing
what it feels like to try to act like nothing ever happened, despite
hearing, "Good thing you weren't going down the stairs—that could
have been *really* dangerous!" (I wasn't amused either.) Not all of
your blunders are as bad as you think they are. Don't get hung up
on things you can't change or control; just let it go!

MY MOST EMBARRASSING MOMENT

*The flight was departing Washington, D. C. I look forward to
flying out of D.C. because I usually meet interesting people. For this
reason (and to make myself feel better) I try to look respectable. This
flight was no exception. During the boarding process, I decided to use
the spacious restroom in First Class.*

*I learned a valuable lesson on this flight: You must never forget to
securely lock the restroom door! There I was, minding my own business.
As the door of the "occupied" restroom flew open, I quickly looked down*

to see very expensive Italian shoes. As if in slow motion, my eyes moved upward catching every thread, crease, monogram, and lapel pin. Eventually, my eyes made contact with those of a United States Senator. His face was a patriotic red as he quickly slammed the restroom door shut. I locked it and immediately went into panic mode.

I didn't move. Despite repeated requests from the flight attendant to return to my seat, I stayed put until the pilot finally "requested" I take my seat. Pulling myself together, I left the security of the restroom. What were the odds that the Senator and I were seated together anyways? *I naively thought on my way back to my seat.*

Oh, yes! My travel companion and I had met earlier. He sat reading his Wall Street Journal (upside down) and I quietly said, "Excuse me," as I took my seat. He never looked up. He never said a word. What exactly did I expect him to say, "Nice to see you again"? I picked up my book and started reading. It was over. I let it go.

Principle Three: I'm O.K. You're O.K.

I've already established that I'm short. This doesn't mean I always wanted to be short. In fact, I've always wanted to be ten inches taller. I'd look thinner and could find my way out an exit door in a crowded theatre without having to hold onto my husband's shirt. But in reality, I am vertically challenged at five feet plus a quarter-inch. This is the way it is. Improving your ZQ is not a sign of weakness or criticism. It is evidence of your desire to be better, smarter, and happier. Have enough self-esteem to welcome evaluation, criticism, and praise.

Principle Four: Do not expect different results by repeating the same behaviors.

As simple as this may sound, it's worth pointing out the obvious. In order to enhance, improve, increase, and change your current charismatic potential, you need to start behaving and thinking differently. You can't say you want to go from being a C student to an A student and then use the same study habits that got you all those C grades. You can't say (and I've tried) you are "officially dieting" and sit on the couch watching ESPN workout programs while eating a bag of potato chips. Change requires you do something differently than you are currently doing; whether by adding, revising, or deleting, it is now your job to leave your comfort zone and experiment. Are you ready to *Zing!* your life and leadership?

THE FACTOR OF READINESS

The degree to which you are not only prepared to think about incorporating, deleting, and revisiting attitudes and behaviors that have brought you to this point, but are also willing to act on this knowledge, will determine just how influential you can become. You need to be motivated from the inside out. Otherwise, you will find yourself placing responsibility for the outcome on those you perceive to have caused your effort, as opposed to owning your goal. Don't try to *Zing!* because other people think you should or because you might lose your job if you don't. Motivational strategies only work when they mean something to you. The time to start the process of change begins when you are ready to begin.

MOTIVATIONAL STRATEGIES

To sum up in a few sentences what you need to be motivated to change is comparable to asking a travel agent to get the cheapest flight possible to the Bermuda without telling him what airport you will be departing from! Use those effective motivational strategies that work for you. Unless you really want to achieve happiness, nothing I can say will make you happy. You've got to want it. You've got to recognize the need or void in your life and make a decision to change.

A "kick in the seat of your pants" never hurt anyone, however, and I can't help but suggest the following inspirational techniques for self-motivation:

1. Enlist the support of a friend to go through the journey with you.
2. Get a calendar or journal to record one step you are taking every day—for thirty days—to become more charismatic.
3. Identify someone to serve as your coach and follow your progress.
4. Set small, obtainable goals and reward yourself upon

accomplishment of each goal.
5.   Surround yourself with inspirational books and posters
      of people you admire.
6.   Read Chapter 12 on attitude.

TRIGGER PHRASES FOR ACTION

In *Reawakening Your Passion for Work*, Richard Boyatiz, Annie McKee, and Daniel Goleman identify six "trigger" phrases clearly signaling it's time to make necessary changes in your life. Have you spoken any of the following phrases lately?

"I feel trapped."
"I'm bored."
"I'm not the person I want to be."
"I won't compromise my ethics."
"I can't ignore the call."
"Life is too short."

These statements cover a wide host of situations, from being in volunteer positions that no longer challenge your talents to experiencing the untimely death of a friend's child. Think about some of the more frustrating situations you've found yourself in recently. If you had been better able to override competing forces (i.e. boss' temper, colleague's competitiveness, daughter's teenage rebellion, and so on) to positively influence others, would you have produced a more desirable outcome?

A DIALOGUE OF ONE

In addition to the list of six trigger phrases above, consider your "internal talk." Have you thought any of the following thoughts lately?

I don't have any close friends.
I don't like the friends I do have.
My dog won't play with me.
I feel old.
People don't seem to notice me.
I feel unappreciated.

People around me are happier than I am.
I don't look my best.
I find little enjoyment in what I do on a daily basis.
There's always tomorrow.
I used to be fun to be around.
Maybe Dr. Phil will have the answer.
Why does this always happen to me?
I've fallen and I can't get up.

THE PROCESS OF CHANGE

Self-improvement or personal development is risky: you might just get what you want! As the following chart illustrates, change occurs in a process. The Denney Comfort Zone Chart describes the risks associated with change, which direction your arrow of energy is going, and the types of behaviors you assume during the process of change. This is not a theory of how change occurs; rather, what you experience as you change. It allows you to identify and accept the reality that change makes you different—causing a different response by others. (Isn't that the point?) Change makes others need to figure out what you are doing and why you are doing it.

DENNEY COMFORT ZONE CHART

Zone	Types of Behaviors	Perceived by Others	Focus	Risk Level
Comfort Zone	Habits	Predictable	You	Little\ None
Transition Zone	New Skills	Unpredictable	Changing	Moderate
Exploration Zone	New Habits and New Skills	Influential	Others	High

COMFORT ZONE

Like the pair of slippers you refuse to throw away, the Comfort Zone represents safety. Here you know what you know and accept what you are willing to accept about yourself. This is reality according to you. Others treat you based upon their assumptions of your patterned behaviors and attitudes. M. Scott Peck says, "Your life is the sum-total of the choices you have made." In the Comfort Zone, you have chosen to live with who you've become—the good, bad, and ugly. Some parts of your life are exciting, but the parts you could be changing aren't being changed.

TRANSITION ZONE

In the Transition Zone you are acting on becoming different. You have made a decision to move on and, in some cases, move out! You are willing to risk the security of The Comfort Zone for a better life and more productive leadership. You want success and happiness and are willing to take action. People aren't sure how to react to you, however, because you are showing them "something new." In this zone, you begin to communicate more effectively. You make others feel better about themselves in your presence by increasing the rate you compliment them. You are more flexible to others' desires, and actively look for ways to be considerate to others. Those accustomed to your lack of interest in their lives, for example, might not trust the "new" you. Be patient. Consistency of your behaviors will build their trust over time.

EXPLORATION ZONE

This zone is your goal. You want to live your life and leadership in a continual state of self-assessment and self-development. In this outermost zone, others recognize your efforts in very positive ways. You feel comfortable with risk-taking and your risks have been paying off. Your scope of influence is increasing. You have acquired more effective skills. You overcome previous obstacles to your effectiveness because you can identify and deal with them. You are more confident. People have begun to treat you differently and are more impressed by your ideas. You are not only getting what you want, but you are thinking beyond what you've already got to a wider range of possibilities.

You sincerely believe you can get whatever you want when you focus on *giving* to others. This level of "charismatic contentment" is reflected in others' perceptions of your positive intentions to make the world a better place—one person at a time. Remember, it's not about you; it's about them! You are alive. You are happy. You *Zing!*

BRING IT ON

It's time. Enough talk. Enough words. Change only happens when you act and it's time to act. You are twenty-one insights away from knowing and being a better you. The assessment for each insight is found in Appendix A: Chapter Self-Assessments. Take time to consider the various opportunities for achieving greater personal clarity and truth. Your ability to lead is directly related to your ability to live a happy and meaningful life. When you lead, you live!

"I believe that the rendering of useful service is the common duty of mankind and that only in the purifying fire of sacrifice is the dross of selfishness consumed and the greatness of the human soul set free."
— John D. Rockefeller, Jr.

5

Insight One:
The Opportunity For
Self-Inspection

*"In this world the one thing supremely worth having is the
opportunity to do well and worthily a piece of work of
vital consequence to the welfare of mankind."*
—Theodore Roosevelt

When you put on a pair of overalls, you are ready to overhaul
just about anything! Similarly, when your office gets a new document shredder, papers that were once significant are now dispos-
able. When your neighbor gets a twenty-five cubic foot dumpster, you
go to bed thinking of things to discretely toss in it! Whether a pair
of overalls, document shredder, or large dumpster, opportunities
will arrive in your life, daring you to evaluate what's important,
useful, underused, insignificant, or overrated.

In the early 1990s, leadership experts and researchers Warren
Bennis and Robert J. Thomas interviewed an assortment of leaders
in search of common characteristics of leadership. Their research
revealed the role of "reflective structures."[1] Specifically, successful
leaders had a collection of similar traits, including time and space
allocated for self-examination. For some individuals, this translated
as daily exercise; for others, religious prayer. Some leaders took
"sabbaticals;" others took numerous "mini-vacations." How you
choose to remove yourself from distraction to allow for personal
questioning and soul-searching doesn't matter. The important thing
is that you get in the habit of spending time focusing inward.

LOOK IN THE MIRROR

Self-inspection is a process of self-discovery. It's not about telling you what you want to hear, but about being truthful. Effective leaders and individuals with *Zing!* constantly seek ways of soliciting feedback about their performance, effectiveness, and areas of needed improvement. They are open to others' opinions of them and are not threatened or intimidated by evaluative measures. Likewise, they know and appreciate the many benefits of being receptive to suggestion or feedback. In return, they give and receive evaluation in an environment free from judgment, personal attacks, and incivility. Evaluation may be uncomfortable, but it doesn't have to be hurtful.

Eleanor Roosevelt once said: "People can't make you feel inferior without your consent." Her statement suggests the power of interpretation and perspective. Have you ever been told "You're not living up to your potential?" Do you remember your reaction? The ability to remove negative emotions from statements (or observations) about your performance is a skill. Instead of becoming defensive, for example, check your emotions. Apply the criticism to a specific behavior. You can change behaviors. Don't miss the benefits because you are too sensitive. Self-examination is an important tool of growth. Refuting the evidence or blaming the evaluator (even if that's you), doesn't make the observation any less true.

THE VALUE OF SELF-EXAMINATION

Self-examination is not free of criticism—or praise. It is important to examine what you do well, as well as how others *receive* your strengths and weaknesses. To *Zing!*, exchange your need to be liked for the higher need of pursuing what really matters: truth. In other words, the benefits of knowing where you excel or need to improve far outweigh the temporary discomforts or nagging, unsubstantiated suspicions held inside.

Because effective leaders continually strive to raise their personal bar of excellence, they also achieve higher levels of excellence. The process of personal examination takes you to a higher place. Others may neither understand nor appreciate the value in self-examination, which includes:

- Achieving a more accurate perception of what others find appealing and not appealing
- Improving your potential to have better interpersonal relationships
- Allowing you to be less defensive and more sensitive to others' needs
- Enhancing your confrontation skills
- Strengthening your self-confidence
- Role-modeling strong character and desire for self-improvement
- Making you more approachable (especially by subordinates)
- Making you a better student of life and leadership
- Enhancing your skills of assessment
- Allowing you to capitalize on your strengths and minimize your weaknesses
- Helping you to re-direct your energies toward areas of greater need

When you are in a continual state of self-actualization, you are in a continual state of growth and development. This can keep you alive and moving forward. Human growth and development require a constant look in the mirror. To do nothing as the world changes around you is to actually lose ground. You are no longer "in style." You risk not living up to your potential the day you believe you have already maximized it!

LIKE RIDING A BIKE

Albeit uncomfortable, evaluation is not new to you. In your youth, you handed in an assignment and it came back with a letter grade. The more diligent you were in completing your homework or the greater your effort, the higher the grade, or reward, you received.

In Spanish, "Duerme la cabeza" translates to English as "I have a headache." I know this because my elementary Spanish teacher, Senorita Schneider, gave any student who correctly spoke this phrase two M&Ms to make their "headache" go away (I love M&Ms). My elementary art teacher, Ms. Uffer, rewarded my love of painting by allowing me to wash paintbrushes and help clean up after every class. In college, letter grades didn't matter to me. It was about the numbers. Right or wrong, external rewards (like candy or cleaning) weren't as important as the digits. In fact, the slightest increase in a single tenth of a decimal point was significant to my GPA (and many of my peers'). Consequently, I (along with my peers) created anxiety over grades. Instead of looking forward to the many benefits of being more knowledgeable, I agonized over specific numbers and grading techniques. (Have you ever had the "I didn't study for the exam" nightmare?) Getting graded was all part of the deal, but it wasn't "the" deal. Evaluation is a reward of self-discovery.

REALITIES OF SELF-ASSESSMENT

Below is a list of legitimate reasons people tend to resist self-examination or postpone it. Some, or all, of the list may apply to you. By making you aware of these reasons in advance, you can accept and/or deal with them one by one. You can expect them as part of the process. How are you going to address the following realities of self-examination?

- Leads to more insecurity
- Feeds an already weak sense of self
- Requires a new skill set
- Leaves you feeling vulnerable with the person sharing the information
- Opens wounds better left covered
- Terrifies you
- Ignites feelings of being rejected or dismissed
- Forces you to do something with the information offered

GROW IN CONFIDENTIALITY

Have you ever met anyone who shared his or her entire life history in the first five minutes of conversation? You walked away thinking *that was more information than I needed to know.* When you build "reflective structures" into your daily life and leadership, you will collect information from you and for you. Honor your right to privacy. Respect others' rights to their privacy. Just because someone asks you about personal matters does not mean you have to share them. I recommend that you keep the results of self-assessments (or any kind of evaluation) to yourself unless you are sharing the information for developmental purposes. If so, then only share what makes you feel comfortable.

SKILL BUILDING LESSON

1. Go to Appendix A and complete the self-assessment titled "On Self-Assessment."
2. Spend fifteen minutes a day observing others' behaviors. Write down what you found appealing and/or not appealing. Compare these behaviors to your own.
3. For 14 consecutive days, schedule an activity of self-reflection in which you give yourself time and space to contemplate your ability to handle what that day brings. This could be a bike ride, walk around the block, writing in a journal, meditation, and so on.
4. Go to your bookstore and pick up three self-help books that focus on those parts of your life that you need to improve. Read them.
5. Listen quietly the next time someone tries to tell you something about your attitude or behavior. Refrain from making any response other than to re-iterate what you hear them trying to tell you.
6. Focus on potential "signs" providing feedback about your *Zing!* Quotient. For example, are you left out of certain discussions? Do people avoid making eye contact with you?
7. Be willing to risk hearing the truth. Solicit comments about your personality from friends, co-workers, and even complete strangers.
8. Consider hiring a coach or counselor to assist you in translating or processing your self-discoveries.

"Have you learned lessons only of those who admired you, and were tender with you, and stood aside for you? Have you not learned great lessons from those who rejected you, and braced themselves against you, or disputed passage with you?"
—Walt Whitman

6

Insight Two: The Content of Character

"There are those who believe something, and therefore tolerate nothing; and on the other hand, those who tolerate everything, because they believe nothing."
—*Robert Browning*

One of the most inspirational places to stand in all of America is at the foot of the Lincoln Memorial in Washington, D. C. Standing in front of Abraham Lincoln you are inspired to never tell another lie—regardless of how small. I'm not sure why, but something about his enormous, concrete presence inspires truthfulness. Perhaps his magnetic pull originates with the image of "Honest Abe" taught to us when we were young. Unfortunately, we grow up and forget this internal source of self-respect: truthfulness.

Leadership authority and motivational speaker, Brian Tracy, identified in his bestselling book *Create Your Own Future*, the twelve critical factors of unlimited success. Like other leadership resources, he included the role of character. Tracy contends, "The universal truth is that you inevitably attract into your life the people, circumstances, ideas, opportunities, and resources that are in harmony with your dominant thoughts. You can never achieve on the outside what you have not earned on the inside."

Content of Character

Content of character is the essence of who you are when all of your possessions are gone. It is represented in the *person* part of your *Zing!* Impact Equation. To find your content of character, stand in a room alone and ask yourself if you like the company. Then ask, "Why or why not?" You are either an honest person or not? You can't be true to your content of character if you lie only once in a while, plagiarize only once per term paper, or take only a few things from the office. Dishonesty is dishonesty. Cheating is cheating. Stealing is stealing. How much or how often is irrelevant. You either live your life according to a set of moral standards or not? You are either an honest person or not? Abraham Lincoln once said: "If I can not trust you with the small things, don't expect me to trust you with the big things."

QUESTIONS OF CHARACTER

Questions of character are private. You ask, then answer them internally before you act or speak. For example, "Am I capable of deception, deceit, and/or dishonesty?" "Do I take advantage of situations because I can?" Admitting to these things in front of others isn't going to necessarily change your behavior. Begin your internal dialogue today. Consider the following list of questions of character:

What is the motivation behind my request?
Why do I need to say this right now?
Am I acting out of self-gain or for the benefit of the group?
What other information do I need to make this decision?
What will be the consequences of my actions?
Am I breaking any laws?
Is this ethical?
Am I being true to my morals and values?
WWJD? (What would Jesus do?)

APPLIED INTEGRITY

Your goal is to have a congruent content of character. In other words, what you say and believe in is consistent with what you do. I call this congruency *applied integrity*. Applied integrity is linked to the fundamental concepts of honesty, ethical behavior, values, and moral beliefs. Your actions speak to your values and your values drive your actions. Applied integrity lives at the core of your content of character. Your ability to "walk the walk" and "talk the talk" is so readily apparent to others that its absence creates disconnect—or distance—between you and your ability to influence others.

Individuals with *Zing!* demonstrate a visible sense of applied integrity.

COMPONENTS OF CHARACTER

TRUST

The interesting thing about trust is that it takes a long time to build and only seconds to destroy. To build trust is to do what you say you will do – and when you say you will do it. When you practice applied integrity twenty-four hours a day, people give you the benefit of the doubt when discrepancies between your actions and your words arise. They assume that there is another explanation or something out of the ordinary has occurred. In other words, they trust your intentions. Your influence has not been compromised.

If others can't trust you to be who you say you are, then they will suspect everything you do and say. They will question your motives. They will examine your statements carefully. They start looking for ways to verify your statements by bringing other people and sources into your conversations. You will never have *Zing!* if you aren't trustworthy.

EXAMPLE SETTING

Abraham Lincoln also said: "What you do speaks so loud, I cannot hear what you say." Others observe your behavior and draw conclusions based upon that behavior. For example, do you say, "I am a team player" and then proceed to undermine your boss? Do you say, "I want to make the world a better place," and then fail to actively volunteer in your local school, YMCA, and/or hospital? Do you say, "My children and family are the most important things in my life," and then fail to sit down *at least* once a week for a family dinner? The hypocrisy of such character has become the legacy left to our children, and frankly, to our society. Integrity is honesty in action. Demonstrate what you stand for by living it.

MORAL DECISION MAKING

Consider these definitions: "An *unethical decision* is a decision with the pay-off up front. An *ethical decision* is a decision with the pay-off down the line." Sometimes, you do have to "pay your dues," or wait until you've earned what you want. A desire for instant gratification (or wanting more than you deserve) often leads people to be dishonest, cheat, or manipulate a situation to their advantage.

Zing! isn't possible without a strong moral foundation. Rarely do I hear someone say, "I respect you for cheating on your wife," or "I'm in awe of your ability to lie!" Your ZQ goes down every time you cheat, steal someone else's ideas without giving the proper credit, and unfairly take advantage of someone or something. Just because you can get away with it doesn't make it right. Don't worry about anyone else's moral health except your own. That will keep you busy enough.

VALUES

The foundation for your actions is also found in what you hold to be important in life. To answer the question: What matters to you? requires clarity of values. You will be asked many times throughout this book to identify the values guiding your life. From being genuine to generous, loving to laughing, and/or intellectual to inventive, having a clear sense of what matters to you allows you to set priorities accordingly. (A rather complete list of values can be found in Appendix A under Insight Two.)

CONSCIENCE

Causing you to strive for a *Zing!* content of character is the internal dialogue between what you *want* to do and what is the right thing to do. Your conscience never shuts off. Regrettably, it does shut down, however. Avoid making difficult decisions when you are emotionally worn down or overly stressed out. Don't let "peer, fear, or beer pressure" force you to do something you will regret at a later time. And yes, just because everyone else is doing it, doesn't make it right.

THE CONSEQUENCES OF CHARACTER

LITTLE CHARACTER COMES AT A BIG COST

If you show favoritism, conditionally apply morals, waiver on your values, etc., others will notice. Whether as a result of misplaced loyalty or obligation, they may continue to listen to your ideas and take direction from you; however, they do so not because they respect you, but rather because they have to. This is not *charismatic* leadership or *Zing!*; this is positional leadership. When you lack a strong content of character, you need to work harder to build relationships, accomplish tasks effectively, and inspire others to greatness.

A WIN-WIN PROPOSITION

As a result of a *Zing!* content of character, you will feel good about you. You will respect yourself and experience the internal benefits of knowing you care (and love) yourself enough to continually strive to become a better human being. A by-product of your efforts is that others will also admire your high personal standards and many will attempt to meet them. In addition, colleagues, family members, and people you run into on a daily basis will also be more at ease with you because they know what to expect from you. Time and time again, you have proven your good intentions, strong sense of values, and commitment to relationships and/or getting the job done. You will earn the respect of others when you act with character. Respect is a powerful influencing force.

THE RESPONSIBILITY OF LEADERSHIP

Learn right from wrong, then live right. Creating a greater good is (and always has been) inspired by a call to our individual and collective conscience. When I was a little girl playing on my swing set, Dr. Martin Luther King, Jr. was following his call to conscience. On April 4, 1967 he did not stray from his moral sense of obligation to the Civil Rights Movement when he spoke out against the war in Vietnam; rather he reiterated his theme: "violence is violence." The following is an excerpt from "Beyond Vietnam" delivered at the Riverside Church.[1]

Finally, as I try to explain for you and for myself the road that leads from Montgomery to this place, I would have offered all that was most valid if I simply said that I must be true to my conviction that I share with all men the calling to be a son of the living God. Beyond the calling of race or nation or creed is this vocation of sonship and brotherhood. Because I believe that the Father is deeply concerned, especially for His suffering and helpless and outcast children, I come tonight to speak for them. This I believe to be the privilege and the burden of all of us who deem ourselves bound by allegiances and loyalties which are broader and deeper than nationalism and which go beyond our nation's self-defined goals and positions. We are called to speak for the weak, for the voiceless for the victims of our nations, for those it calls "enemy," for no document from human hands can make these humans any less our brothers.

SKILL BUILDING LESSON

1. Go to Appendix A and complete the self-assessment titled "Your Content of Character."
2. Read the landmark speeches of Dr. Martin Luther King, Jr. found in *A Call to Conscience*.
3. Visit www.thecharacterinstitute.com.
4. Do what you say you will do and when you say you will do it.
5. Tell the truth. (Especially on the small stuff.)
6. If you tell a lie, admit your mistake.
7. Don't cheat.
8. Never say (or believe): "Everybody else does it, so it's OK."
9. Remember: *What goes around comes around.*
10. Pay your dues; hard work does pay off.
11. Hold yourself to a higher ethical standard than those around you; doing so will give them someone to look up to.
12. Give credit where credit is due.
13. Never cover up for someone else's unethical decision making.

"Ultimately we judge our leaders in a framework of values."
—John W. Gardner

7

INSIGHT THREE:
THE POWER OF PURPOSE

"When a man does not know what harbor he is making for,
no wind is the right wind."
—Seneca

My son Jake loves to fish. I love to fish, too. Until recently, we fished behind our sailboat going out of the harbor into Buzzard's Bay. True sailors, like my husband, don't appreciate fishing. In fact, the only thing a true sailor appreciates is wind. There should be no lines trailing the boat only to get caught in a lobster pot, or (heaven forbid), slow down the boat. Despite our "captain's" hesitation, Jake and I fish off the stern. Actually, Jake fishes and I watch my line.

What is *your* goal? What do *you* want for your life and leadership? What is *your* purpose in life? Without answers to these questions, you might literally find yourself *Zing!*-less! Purpose guides your direction and movement. It is the wind beneath your sails. If you want to *Zing!*, then you must actively (and continuously) have a plan or a destination.

Individuals with *Zing!* are attractive because they move towards something. It doesn't have to be a single "great" thing (such as running a twenty-six mile marathon.) It doesn't have to have an end point (such as building your company or raising ethical children.) However, to positively influence others, you need to get out of bed every day with the desire to be a productive and contributing member of society. You want the day to be different because you live it. You can accomplish anything when you work towards a pre-determined outcome.

EASIER SAID THAN DONE

You can achieve your goals. Although I know this intellectually (and speak about it often), when I see someone actually get what they want, I am inspired. It motivates me to remember my purpose in life and pursue it with more *Zing!*. Things seemingly out of reach don't seem that unobtainable once other people start obtaining them. After all, knowing that effort leads to results is nice. But seeing the results is exciting.

A KID'S DREAM

Until recently, Jake's job was to be a kid. He received allowance just for being a kid. As he grew older, he took on responsibilities. When Jake turned thirteen, I could see that his wants were out-costing his income. This forced him to earn additional cash to pay for the occasional DVD or CD. He worked odd jobs around the house and did yard work. He got what he wanted.

As spring approached, my newly crowned teenager decided that he wanted his own fishing boat—a great idea, I selfishly thought! He turned on the computer, made a flyer, and walked out the door. Upon his return, I asked what he was up to. He smiled and said, "I'm getting a fishing boat!"

I was intrigued.

"How are you going to pay for this fishing boat?"

He replied, "I just started my own lawn-mowing business. It was easy. I made flyers and handed them out to people on our street. I'm going to save up and own a boat by the end of the summer."

My son had a purpose. He also had a plan.

I reviewed Jake's flyer. Based upon the "economical" pricing plan he had advertised, I figured it would be a few summers before my thirteen year old went trolling across the bay for stripers. Then, the phone began ringing. After seeing his work, many of his clients offered him more than he was charging. Word quickly spread around the neighborhood. Jake's client list grew. His price grew. Before Memorial Day, Jake negotiated a loan from his fishing buddy. Together we went to the bank and withdrew his portion of the down payment. Together we purchased our first fishing boat. Jake named it "The Maka." (He recently informed me, however, that his next goal is to buy me out of my half of the boat!)

WANTING ZING!

You have to actively want something in order to achieve it. Despite the role of luck or fate, individuals with *Zing!* have *Zing!* because they want *Zing!* Successful individuals, and those who lead charismatic lives, achieve because they want to achieve. Their lives have meaning because their lives have purpose. Hal Urban, author of *Life's Greatest Lessons*, says, "Living without goals is like going on a trip without a destination. If you don't know where you're going, you'll probably end up nowhere and any road will get you there." Goals are the result of a clearly defined purpose—or direction—in life.

Since the very first paragraph of this book, I've been insisting that happiness matters. Is happiness a goal, or a purpose, or something else? Can you want happiness (like a kid wants a fishing boat) and simply work to get it? Can you want *Zing!* and simply work to get it? Yes. And, that's where you need to begin—at the very beginning with the belief that you can get what you want while making the world a better place. By understanding the roles of philosophy, purpose, and goal setting, you can achieve *Zing!*.

PHILOSOPHY

Philosophy of life defines why you were born. It represents your definition of life (or Life Mission Statement) and the "bottom line" motivation behind your purpose. Philosophy of life is the foundation, or starting point, for all the decisions you make because it answers why you are making the choices you make. Essentially, philosophy of life is found in the things you cherish and love. All the values you deem important are rooted within philosophy. Before you can have purpose, you need to be able to answer the question: *What matters to you?*

I once heard a speaker say, "There are two truly difficult days in our lives. The day we are born and the day we figure out why." I'm happy to report that I'm still figuring out why. Are you? Stop worrying about complicated answers to the meaning *of* life question and focus on the meaning *in* your life! Define your life based upon what matters to you today.

An example of a life philosophy statement is: *Joy matters. When I give joy, I receive joy.* An opportunity to write your personal Life's Philosophy Statement is found in this chapter's self-assessment.

Change your philosophy of life as *you* change. Be content with continual discovery. Your philosophy of life can be altered dramatically through life events, remain the same, or come in and out of focus over time. However, to *Zing!*, you need to know what drives you. From this very specific value statement, your purpose emerges. And from this more specific purpose, an assortment of goals (varying in size and significance) emerges.

PURPOSE

Purpose of life defines what you are trying to achieve—as well as how you achieve it. Deepak Chopra in *The Seven Spiritual Laws of Success* says, "Everyone has a purpose in life…a unique gift or special talent to give to others. And when we blend this unique talent with service to others, we experience the ecstasy and exultation of our own spirit, which is the ultimate goal of all goals." Purpose represents not the power to achieve something, but rather the *will to work* or intention towards something. Indira Gandhi said: "The purpose of life is to believe, to hope, and to strive." Within her words is a larger philosophy of faith, future, and growth.

Purpose is more visible than philosophy. Others can literally "see" your purpose or intention, whereas they "deduce" your philosophy of life. Your purpose is defined by your vocation or how you spend your time, where you put your energies, and toward what end you communicate to others. For example, people observe you teaching, preaching, coaching, or building. They notice you work hard, commit to an organization or employer, and conduct yourself professionally. To build on the previous example of a Life Philosophy Statement, you may define your purpose as: *To bring joy into the lives of children through teaching.*

GOALS

Goal and *purpose* are often used interchangeably. However, I use the term "goal" to represent smaller more practical means of carrying out your larger purpose. Goals allow you to accomplish your purpose, and purpose clarifies your philosophy of life. Goals are even more specific than purpose. They can have a time frame (such as lowering your blood pressure in six months) or be open-ended (such as staying in shape.) Goals necessitate action. To achieve a greater good requires you to set obtainable goals and plan accordingly. The only way to achieve a goal is to determine your acceptable level of risk-taking, develop a plan, and act.

So, if your philosophy of life is: *Joy matters. When I give joy, I receive joy,* and your purpose is: *to bring joy into the lives of children through teaching,* then your goal is: *to get a Master's degree in elementary education.*

OBJECTIVES

Goals are accomplished through objectives. A "To Do" list is an example of a list of objectives. I define *objective* as a short-term and easily measured action or task required to make something larger happen. If you set a goal of enhanced staff synergy, for instance, you accomplish it by establishing a variety of objectives, from team-building exercises to enhancing lines of communication. One objective usually won't get the job done. The more elaborate your goal, the more objectives. Therefore, if you want something, you need to break your goal down into smaller parts or objectives. If you find one approach ineffective, try a different approach. You can change objectives without changing your goals. When I was working full time with two infants, I forgot this rule of thumb. Instead of changing direction, I allowed myself to be continually frustrated. I repeatedly hit my head against the proverbial brick wall, watched the bump on my head grow bigger, yet continued to blame the wall instead of redirecting my energies. You too, have choices when you hit a wall. Alter your approach.

Once you put your objectives in motion, you begin to impact and influence the world around you. When you do positive things, you positively influence. When you do negative things, you negatively influence. *Zing!* means adding to the world—not letting the world pass you by.

Following through on our example, add the following objective to the pattern above: *to take my elementary class on a field trip to the ice cream shop during the last week of school.*

CLEARLY ARTICULATE YOUR PURPOSE

Philosophy, purpose, goals, and objectives—when clarified in that order, can provide the destination and road map for your life and leadership. You don't set out to make your philosophy come true, but your philosophy determines your purpose and goals. Is your life and leadership representative of *why* you are on the planet?

SKILL BUILDING LESSON

1. Go to Appendix A and complete the self-assessment titled "Life Mission Statement."
2. Make a list of all the things that truly matter to you.
3. Review the list of values offered in the Appendix A under "Insight Two." Identify the common thread that runs throughout. Why do they matter?
4. Talk about your goals out loud.
5. Break down your purpose into goals and objectives.
6. Ask How? to achieve what you want to achieve, not if it will ever happen.
7. Read about individuals who have accomplished great things.
8. Write your own story in a journal. (We all have a story.)
9. Visit and make a stronger commitment to your spiritual development.
10. Commit yourself to a volunteer activity in your immediate environment or local community.
11. Let go of things that don't matter so you have room for what counts.
12. Set deadlines. Self-imposed deadlines can easily be overlooked, so employ or enlist another external source to enforce your deadline.

"I shall pass this way but once; any good, therefore, that I can do or any kindness that I can show to any human being, let me do it now. Let me not defer or neglect it, for I shall not pass this way again"
—Christopher Jachimowicz

8

Insight Four:
The Inspiration of Vision

"The consideration that human happiness and moral duty are inseparably connected will always continue to prompt me to promote the former by inculcating the practice of the latter."
—George Washington

My daughter wants to be President of the United States. She has been patriotic since the day she was born...the Fourth of July! Fireworks on her birthday seem appropriate. Kaitlin always talks about living in the White House. She sees a peaceful world in her lifetime and believes world leaders should talk instead of fight. She also believes one person can make a difference.

In preparation for her run for the White House, Kaitlin loves history and writing. Even at the age of twelve, she has expressed a desire to attend Harvard or Yale. Having studied all of the previous presidents, she does not wish to be the *first* female president. She'd prefer other females to "break through" so that she can worry about running the country instead of running an uphill battle. Because of Kaitlin's clearly articulated vision, her friends have already "called" certain cabinet positions. Her Chief of Staff will be her enthusiastic best friend Mary. To date, no men are included in *her* White House...

Vision Defined

Vision differs from purpose because vision is "pie in the sky" thinking. It's dreamlike. Purpose is practical. Vision is the ability to see what isn't there with mystic clarity. Purpose is a guide. Vision is a unique ability routinely found in effective leaders, entrepreneurs, and difference-makers.

THE BENEFITS OF VISION

Walt Disney said: "If you can dream it, you can achieve it." All too often we tend to "play it safe" and not risk the ridicule or self-humiliation of being labeled a "dreamer." What's wrong with being a dreamer? Without individuals to see things before they created them, we wouldn't have bridges, electric cars, and ipods! We wouldn't have penicillin. Michelangelo wouldn't have painted the Sistine Chapel. Ted Turner wouldn't have created CNN and Bill Gates wouldn't have developed an operating system that revolutionized personal computers. Without the ability to look beyond what's already been done, these two charismatic individuals wouldn't have joined together to inoculate third world countries. Bill Gates and Ted Turner have *Zing!*.

CHARACTERISTICS OF VISIONARY THINKERS

Many leadership experts identify the ability to "clearly articulate a vision for the future" as the one differentiating trait between effective leaders and exceptional leaders. The research on charismatic traits and follower effects by Conger and Kanungo support these conclusions. "Charismatic leaders differ from other leaders by their ability to formulate and articulate an inspirational vision and by exhibiting actions that create an impression that they and their mission are extraordinary."[1] You can go beyond your day to day thinking when you are willing to assume the following traits of visionary thinkers:

FREE THINKERS

Free thinkers are magnetic because they see something others don't or have chosen not to see. They think outside the box while others color inside the lines. They create new ways of approaching a desired outcome by examining what needs to be accomplished. They are not only free thinkers; they are free to think. Give yourself permission to direct a desired outcome by envisioning that outcome with enthusiasm. What do you want to see?

PROACTIVE

Visionary thinkers anticipate obstacles in advance. If you know who will resist your efforts, what resources will be needed, what policies might interfere with your plans, you can incorporate the overcoming of them in your planning process. Continually think down the road and do what you need to do now to be ready.

RISK-TAKERS

Go beyond the safety nets of what others expect to hear and engage them in a fantasy you intend to make reality. You may fail. Hank Aaron holds the record for hitting the most home runs as a professional baseball player. He is number two in the record books for the most strikeouts. Be willing to go to bat.

STAY FOCUSED ON THE CAUSE

What can you do to keep your "eye on the ball?" Visionary thinkers surround themselves with reminders of what they are trying to achieve. For example, chairman of Starbuck's Corp, Howard Schutlz is described in *Business Leaders and Success* as staying true to his mission by digging his hands into a bin of freshly roasted coffee beans, and then taking a big whiff. The strong aroma revives Schultz's original passion for the business. Schutlz is quoted as confirming: "[Putting my hands in coffee beans] helps me remember how we got started and what we need to sustain, you have to go back to the cause—which in our case is the coffee. It's our love of coffee."

Other ways of keeping your vision in front of you include placing a chart depicting desired earnings on your office wall, a photo of smiling children on your bookcase, or an architectural drawing of a marina you will own and operate. What represents or symbolizes your vision(s)?

BELIEVE IN THEMSELVES AND THEIR IDEAS

According to Dr. Tony Alessandra in *Charisma*, "Charismatic people possess a similar, almost childlike faith in their vision and their ability to create change. People will follow leaders whose vision inspires them and makes their lives more meaningful." It's not enough to merely wish the homeless fed, a cure for cancer found, or more children taught how to read; you need to visualize your dreams and desires so they turn into obtainable goals. It's worth repeating: *you can achieve that which you imagine to be real.*

RESOURCEFUL

You will be more visionary than your beige counterparts if you can point out more than one way of hitting a target—a target you clearly see in your mind. Your resourcefulness provides others with hope, direction, and enthusiasm for the future. Visionary thinkers frequently ask: *How can my talents, time and energy make my part of the world a better place?* Look intensely at what is at your disposal before determining you don't have what it takes to make the world a better place. You do. In addition, be ready when opportunity knocks. Corporate icon and talk show host Oprah Winfrey suggests, "Luck is a matter of preparation meeting opportunity." Create your luck.

ASSOCIATE WITH VISIONARY THINKERS

Who wants to be involved with what you are doing? Who follows your lead? More importantly, whose lead do you follow? Vision is often shaped by your associations and environments of opportunity. High achievers, for example, attract other high achievers. Underachievers seek out other underachievers. If you want to achieve your dreams, associate with people who achieve their dreams.

SKILL BUILDING LESSON

1. Go to Appendix A and complete the self-assessment titled "Making Vision Reality."
2. Think outside of the box for the tasks you have to accomplish today. (Creative and divergent thinking is discussed in Chapter Eleven.)
3. Think about your future.
4. Visualize your life in five years.
5. Continually discuss your vision. Share it with others.
6. Keep your vision in front of you. Use visual reminders of what you want or have already set out to achieve.
7. Encourage others to articulate their visions.
8. Study the great visionary thinkers of the 21st century.
9. Ask every child you meet what they want to be when they grow up.

MY DREAMS: BOTH BIG AND SMALL

By Kaitlin Elizabeth Denney (Age 12)

Be the president of the United States.
Write and publish a novel by the time I'm twenty-five years old.
Get into my first choice college.
Be on the National Honor Society list at least once.
Travel to a different continent and see how other people in the
world live.
Save someone's life in any way.
Be someone's role model.
Inspire someone.
Meet someone I love and marry him.
Learn to appreciate what I have.
Become a novelist.
Make sure the people around me know how much I love them.
Be a creator of surprise.
Help those who need it, whenever humanly possible.
Never hate myself, but always love myself.
Remember that what other people think is important.
Be a leader in my own eyes.
Never give up on my dreams.

9

Insight Five:
The Transcending of Adversity

"Life is like a window. Sometimes you have to look through the pain to see the view."
—Randolph Macon college student

When you are a college student, you get to engage in behaviors otherwise thought to be immature by traditional social standards. You get to stay up all night IMing (instant messaging) your friends across the hall. You get to save all of your dirty laundry until vacation time, when you bring it home to mom. When you are a college student, you can think it's acceptable to wear your pajamas to class, greet people you saw two hours earlier with a big hug, and make strange noises in a crowd of like-minded people, provoking unstoppable laughter. Male or female, college students can be rather playful individuals.

The U.S. Census Bureau reports that less than 30% of the United States' population has a two or four-year college degree. However, the idea of "college" is widely understood. College students go to class, do homework, study and graduate. For some, this privilege is assured. For others, it is an unobtainable goal. The roadblocks (or competing forces) preventing millions of Americans from pursuing higher education range from lacking encouragement to lacking financial resources; for many, the forces working *against* them are insurmountable compared to the resources available *to* them.

ADVERSITY DEFINED

Adversity is challenge. It represents a powerful or competing force of resistance to you or your mission. Adversity comes in many shapes and sizes. Sometimes we create the adversity in our lives.

Other times, adversity happens. Adversity can be real or perceived. Either way, it represents to you that which you haven't conquered (in one form or another), yet must conquer to move forward in your life and leadership. Examples of adversity include: losing your job, lacking start up capitol, being diagnosed with cancer, growing up poor, losing your eyesight, lacking a supportive family, discrimination, ignorance, and taking care of an aging parent or sick child. Rich, poor, tall, short, young, or old: to be human is to face adversity at some point in your life.

Not all adversity needs to be interpreted or received as negative. In fact, exceptional leaders are often defined by their ability to turn the adversity in their lives into character-building opportunities. They have learned the very difficult lesson of acceptance. Instead of being ashamed, embarrassed, victimized, or controlled by the difficult (or devastating) events in their lives, individuals with *Zing!* accept them as part of their history, or makeup.

In the Eyes of the Beholder

I grew up in a college town. Both of my parents were college professors. My friends' parents were also college professors. I learned at an early age that most college students will seek any opportunity to have fun or be a tad wacky. Most of their fun is innocent enough…

From the time I was about eight years old until I went to high school at the age of fourteen, my three sisters and I walked over a mile to our elementary school and then home for lunch. On good days, our father met us at the corner and joined our mid-day break. I say on "good days" because, when we were not protected by his presence, we became targets of "college boys just wanting to have fun."

Our walking route included passing one of the local fraternity houses. On sunny days, the frat boys found enjoyment in chucking water balloons at moving targets—including passing cars, low flying birds, and cute little girls like my sisters and me. Being prospective engineers, their projection devices were rather impressive. I still remember the feeling of gearing up mentally to pass the fifty feet of sidewalk identified as the "target zone." After awhile, my sisters and I became rather proficient in avoiding balloon contact, as well as eliminating the fear of being hit. After all, it was only water (or beer).

OVERCOMING ADVERSITY MEANS MAKING A CHOICE

My feelings about adversity have changed over the years. I've learned you can't always run away from it. The internal dilemma of dealing with adversity, however, has remained rather constant. Adversity, whether in the form of a water balloon, significant obstacle, challenge, struggle, physical disability, personal tragedy, national crisis, loss, or lack of opportunity, forces you to make decisions. You have to decide what you are going to do about your situation. Overcoming adversity begins with a choice to move forward.

Early in her career, Oprah Winfrey had to overcome being a victim of child abuse to become a television reporter. College president Dr. Maureen Hartford had to overcome being a woman in a predominately male field to become one of a handful of high ranking female CEOs in higher education. Professor Dr. Joe Martin had to overcome being told he wasn't "college material" to become one of the youngest college professors in the country. Children's author and speaker Johnny Tuitel had to overcome what the world considered "normal" or "perfect" to marry the woman of his dreams, and father three great kids despite his physical disability.

A COMMON BOND

Every human being on the planet lives with adversity. And, every human being handles adversity differently. My adversity might seem insignificant to your adversity because my life has been different than your life. To become overwhelmed, or resort to ineffective coping mechanism (substance abuse, inflicting abuse on others, withdrawing socially, and so on) when adversity knocks at your door, is to deny the fact: *life is difficult*. These three words are also the first three words in M. Scott Peck's bestseller *A Road Less Traveled*. Throughout his book, Peck paints an insightful picture of life containing a series of highs and lows. To ignore the lows makes it hard to celebrate the highs.

Likewise, I know from my own history that not experiencing adversity until later in life leaves you limited in your emotional response. I was blessed to grow up never having dealt with significant adversity until my husband's cancer. I hadn't had any "practice" using the insight of adversity, so I fell hard and fast. It took me a considerable amount of time and effort to recapture a sense of emotional stability. The experience taught me, however, that you can't tell someone it will "all be OK" because you don't know that. It also taught me bad things happen to good people and life isn't fair. It is in the handling of adversity that your ZQ either rises or falls. Adversity represents *competing forces* in the *Zing!* Impact equation.

LEARNING AND TEACHING FOR A GREATER GOOD

You cross paths with people all the time and never really know them. You might get the benefits of someone's life experience (the good and the bad) without knowing how (or why) he or she is able to influence the world in such a positive (and extraordinary) way. One remarkable woman I've had the honor of getting to know is a very intelligent and caring single parent of two, teacher, and licensed minister. From the outside you see confidence, commitment, excellence, talent, and compassion. You see an incredible ability to counsel others and teach not only subject, but life, to her students, colleagues, and community members.

What you don't see is her life story filled with adversity (the catalyst for her understanding and insight). As a child, this women experienced many significant hardships. When she was celebrating her sixth birthday, her eleven year old brother was killed by a drunk driver on his way to school. Soon afterwards, her father was seriously injured on the job, and consequently, her family of thirteen experienced going from middle class to poor. During this time she was also sexually molested.

In her adult life, this influential difference maker overcame significant attitudes and prejudices against female pastors, divorce, economic pressures forcing her to work three jobs to support her family, jealousy, self-doubt, and physical and mental exhaustion.

How did she find her way to inspire so many? Despite being tracked in remedial English in 8th grade (because of her sibling's academic reputations), a teacher noticed her intellectual ability and encouraged her to pursue her intellectual development. Her academic confidence built throughout high school. She faced the desire (and ability) to go to college for Elementary Education without any financial assistance and a discouraging high school guidance counselor. From college she studied in seminary school (where she faced additional discrimination) and became a full-time public school educator. Her goal is to pursue a

Master's and Doctorate degree in Educational Leadership and/or Counseling.

After learning of the adversity my friend has overcome in her lifetime, I asked her how she defines "success" and "happiness." She said, "Success is when the words spoken about you or the thoughts remembered about you are lovingly passed around while eliciting the same intensity of warmth and respect they first created." Her next response speaks to her understanding of adversity, "Happiness is being content in any given situation. When I am in a difficult challenge... I am assured and content that it will pass. This realization enables me to live beyond the boundaries and expectations that can influence my actions and reaction to a given situation."

THE PROCESS OF OVERCOMING ADVERSITY

Overcoming adversity requires you to accept that which you can't change and to change the things under your control. It also underscores the ability of one person (such as an 8th grade English teacher) to positively influence another human being. One person can make a difference. You also learn from the true story above that charismatic individuals free themselves emotionally to deal with adversity in a proactive and productive manner. They move forward.

THE GRID OF ADVERSITY

I've created a grid to put the complexities of adversity into perspective. You begin the process of transcending adversity by determining two things: first, who or what created the adversity; and second, when it was created.

WHO CREATED THE ADVERSITY?

	IN YOUR CONTROL	OUT OF YOUR CONTROL
	(CHOICES YOU MAKE)	*(LIFE)*
Past	You leave an argument unresolved.	A parent/significant other abandons you.
	You quit your job.	Your company is downsized.
	You spend more money than you make.	Credit card interest rates climb.
	You do not exercise.	You are born with diabetes.
	You move away from home.	Your house burns down.
	RESPONSE = MANAGE ADVERSITY	*RESPONSE = ACCEPT ADVERSITY*
Present	Fear of commitment	Your parents' divorce
	Failure to communicate with your boss	Corporate culture
	Living over your means	Cost of living
	Being overweight and out of shape	Rising medical expenses
	Significant credit card debt	Alan Greenspan (interest rates)
	RESPONSE = ELIMINATE ADVERSITY	*RESPONSE = INSURE AGAINST ADVERSITY*

(left margin: TIME FRAME)

WHICH RESPONSE FITS YOUR LIFE?

The four responses below correspond to one of the four squares in the Grid of Adversity above. To be helpful, first identify which square best fits the adversity (if any) in your life. Find the response recommended in that square (RESPONSE =). Then, read the fitting response below. (A blank grid is provided in Appendix A, under Insight Five.)

RESPONSES TO ADVERSITY

MANAGE YOUR EXPOSURE.

The source of your adversity is you. As a result of something you did, said, created, or believed in the past, you are still letting the adversity control you! The past isn't going anywhere, but you can! By continually improving your communication skill-set, for example, you can better equip yourself to effectively listen, confront, manage conflict, and articulate your vision. You can spend some time figuring out where you went wrong and what, if anything, you need to do to regain a sense of control over your destiny. If possible, bring closure to unresolved conflicts. If they aren't resolvable, learn to let them go! Don't continually blame others for your shortcomings.

TRANSFER YOUR EXPOSURE.

Are you good at letting those who truly care about you, do so? When situations arise that are not of your own doing, seek a greater faith. Live one day at a time, and give yourself time to process the challenges of the past. Often, feelings of helplessness arise when recovering from adversity. Be willing to ask for help. Seek counseling. Reduce your sources of added pressure until you are in a better position to handle them. Another strategy is to practice forgiveness. Individuals with *Zing!* are not angry, resentful, unproductive, depressed, or withdrawn. They don't lash out, have highs and lows, or sabotage others' good intentions. The best lesson adversity teaches us is how to handle it.

ELIMINATE YOUR EXPOSURE.

When the adversity reflects unfinished business on your part, relationships that bring you down, inadequate health and fitness, low self-esteem, or a fear of taking risks, it's time to either fix the problem or let it go. Move on. You can't recreate or change the past, so focus on the present. Seek counseling, if needed. Work through the consistent patterns of dysfunction, failed relationships, unhappiness, stress and poor job performance, or lack of opportunity. (Remember, *you* are the one common denominator in the equation.) Do what you need to do to improve your skills, adjust your attitude, get back in shape, and have a higher sense of self-worth. If you constantly create the adverse situations in your life and leadership, look in the mirror. Eliminate your exposure. Turn the wrong into a right. This is often accomplished by the humble words "I'm sorry." Saying "I'm sorry" opens more doors than saying "I'm right."

INSURE AGAINST YOUR EXPOSURE.

Put strategies in place to assist you in dealing with situations currently out of your control, as well as those that might suddenly arise. Charismatic individuals take a *proactive* approach to the realities that may present themselves instead of being reactionary. Be willing to adjust your priorities, think differently, and be comfortable with risk-taking. Continually surround yourself with competent individuals and be present for others. They will, in turn be present for you. Building a support network before you need one ensures you'll have what you need when you need it.

SKILL BUILDING LESSON

1. Go to Appendix A and complete the self-assessment titled "Picture This."
2. Deal with your adversity. Don't ignore it or hope it will simply disappear.
3. Yell "Help!" when you need it.
4. Seek professional counseling when you need support.
5. Be willing to let your friends, and loved ones, love you.
6. Write down the potential lessons on life you could learn through overcoming adversity.
7. Look around. How much do you really know about the adversity your neighbors, friends, and colleagues have overcome?
8. Go to motivational lectures or read motivational books.
9. When you drive, put in a motivational CD.
10. Hug strangers if they look like they need one.
11. Hug your friends and family more.

Prayer of Serenity

*Lord, grant me the serenity to accept the things
I cannot change, courage to change the things that I can,
and the wisdom to know the difference.*

10

INSIGHT SIX:
THE CURIOSITY OF COURAGE

*"I am not afraid of storms for
I am learning how to sail my ship."*
—Louisa May Alcott

As a child, I always thought Lassie was simply asking for a bad day by hanging around Jimmy so much. Episode after episode, this beautiful dog jumped into garbage dumpsters, crawled down dilapidated wells, and climbed up cliffs loaded with mud—all for Jimmy, who couldn't stay out of trouble. If Lassie could do all those things (as well as climb a ladder) you'd think she was smart enough to recognize a walking disaster when she saw one. Jimmy was going to keep getting into trouble, and Lassie was going to keep saving him. I used to yell at the television, "Run, Lassie, run! Get out while you can!"

Curiosity and *courage* are often difficult to separate. Children are born with both. I'm not sure which one we lose first as we grow up. When you observe individuals with *Zing!* you sense both are still intact. To increase your ZQ, you need to keep (or get back) a youthful curiosity and openness to experiment, create, and navigate new waters. You need to be willing to go where others haven't gone or continue reaching for happiness even when bad things happen to good people. You *Zing!* when you don't "play it safe" or "stay the party line." You influence others by daring to blaze a path for others to follow. You achieve the unexpected, surviving where others might not.

THE DEFINITION OF COURAGE

Courage is the ability to rise above personal feeling and private ambition to move forward. It is taking action when others retreat.

67

Courage is not recklessness, however. It is bravery when others are frozen in fear or lost in self-pity. This doesn't mean individuals with *Zing!* are never afraid or have legitimate reason to be sad. In fact, anxiety is a very natural emotion accompanying risk or potential danger, and sadness is a healthy response to loss. To have courage is to accept your fears (and their companion emotions) and move on. To quote Ernest Hemingway: "Courage is grace under pressure."

Courage is the ability to pull from deep within to overcome something you (as opposed to someone else) view as more powerful. For example, one needs courage to overcome a drug habit (i.e. addiction), leave an abusive partner (i.e. dependency), care for an elderly parent that you know is no longer taking care of you (i.e. security), and to not cheat while everyone around you is cheating (i.e. peer pressure).

The Pros of Courage

Movement
On the positive side, courage allows you to survive. Courage also allows you to advance a cause, challenge your assumptions, and achieve extraordinary accomplishments. Life constantly offers obstacles and challenges. You choose to either retreat or fight. Courage enables you to respond productively and constructively.

Control
In the absence of courage, you risk losing control over your destiny. Courage allows you to ask for help, seek counseling or guidance, and learn what you need to know to get what you want. One of the greatest benefits of courage is that it teaches you the value of believing in your potential to screw up, mess up, make up, and move on. With courage comes the ability to color with the crayons life gives you (leaving out the beige, of course).

Admiration
Undoubtedly, acts of courage are rewarded with admiration. Acts of courage inspire strength and internal optimism. Whether you realize it or not, your courage is a sign of your faith in the future. You give others hope.

PERSPECTIVE

Your ability to move forward, overcome the odds, or resist temptation is rewarded with the knowledge that you set an example and help those around you to put their own lives in perspective. Although not your intention, your ZQ is raised when you resist fear and act courageously.

THE CONS OF COURAGE

THREATENING TO OTHERS

On the other hand, you may meet (or already know) those who aren't as impressed by your increasing potential to advance your vision simply because your courage brings *their* inadequacies, fears, and defenses to the surface. This doesn't mean you don't have *Zing!*; it means your courage may threaten them.

PRICE TO PAY

Your ability to turn stumbling blocks into stepping stones, set your sites higher than others believe possible, and leave your unpleasant past behind you, for example, might be (and often is) interpreted as "reckless," or creates distrust in your competency. You might lose a few friends for your acts of bravery, be the source of town gossip, and, for no fault of your own, start something that gets out of your control. You will prove people wrong or imply, without intending to, that you have found a better way to live and lead.

Because courage can take many forms, the price you'll pay for being courageous also takes many forms. For instance, telling a bully to leave another kid alone, telling a friend he or she drinks too much and you are taking him/her to a rehab center, or reporting your concerns about the conduct of a high school coach to the principal, are three acts of courage with three potentially different pice tags: a black eye; a life long friendship, or a quick reputation as a trouble maker. The price tag, however, is (or was) rarely a consideration of individuals with remarkable courage. It's not that the consequences don't (or didn't) matter, it's that to not act would have been the far greater tragedy. Consider the lives and leadership of the following: Nelson Mandela, Dr. Martin Luther King, Jr.,

Challenger astronauts (1986), *Columbia* astronauts (2002), Arch Bishop Romero, and the passengers who rushed the cockpit to overcome the terrorists and crash their own plane into the fields of Pennsylvania (September 11, 2001). Never expect great things without a great price tag.

TYPES OF COURAGE

INSTANT COURAGE

Lassie had all kinds of courage. She was forced to act immediately or life was over for Jimmy. She displayed what I call *instant courage*. This is the kind of courage that shows up unexpectedly. You don't have time to think too hard or too long about your response. You often didn't know you had it in you. Examples include your immediate reaction to emergency situations, "final straws," potential harm to others, or "teachable leadership moments."

Have you ever been proud of someone for speaking the right words at the right time? Perhaps they said the same words you wanted to say, but you didn't have the courage to speak up. Have you ever been proud of someone for walking away from a paycheck because his or her employer was unethical? Sometimes it takes instant courage to *not* say or do something.

SUSTAINABLE COURAGE

The other kind of courage is *sustainable courage*. This type of courage often requires sacrifice, diligence, and commitment. It is the hardest kind of courage because it requires physical, emotional, and spiritual energy. You don't take a moment to respond; rather, you take your entire life. How you choose to apply your courage in any scenario will result in reverence.

CHARACTERISTICS OF COURAGE

Would you describe yourself as a courageous individual? Is your ZQ positively or negatively impacted by your responses to adversity? People identified as courageous do the following:

- Focus on others, as opposed to being self-absorbed
- Refrain from the "why me?" attitude
- Avoid blaming others as an excuse for not taking action
- Let go of "unfinished business"
- Keep their faith instead of questioning or abandoning it
- Find faith
- Learn how others have overcome a similar adversity
- Reach out to others by offering empathy
- Make sacrifices with grace
- Seek emotional, physical, and spiritual sources of renewal and energy
- Face their struggles head on, day after day, without giving in to weakness
- Allow themselves to be forgiven
- Let others love them even when they don't feel lovable

PERSONAL PERSPECTIVE ON COURAGE

I call one of my dearest friends "Queenie," albeit a worthy title, her real name is Jean.

Before I relocated two years ago, Her Majesty and I were frequent walking companions. In the earlier years, our conversations were upbeat, humorous, and lighthearted. We talked about our past, present, and future. We talked about what we were going to eat for breakfast, lunch, and dinner. One day, however, the conversations changed. Her son Eddie, was sick. What began as a sore back during a Little League game turned out to be Leukemia.

From that moment on, and for the next four years, the present became our time frame. It was one day at a time. I still looked forward to our walks, but I carried a much heavier heart. My friend, and her family, were living every parent's nightmare. I listened as Jean discussed that day's medical treatments, trips to the doctor's office, and what her other two children and husband were doing after school. For almost four years, and many miles (including a 5K race), Queenie kept to the tasks at hand. She was a loving wife and devoted mother to all three of her children.

Eddie passed away on October 26, 2003 at the age of twelve. The eulogy Jean gave her son as well as, the way she delivered it, summarized

the courageous way she and her family had approached the past four years
of life. Speaking not of what she and her family had lost, but rather
what they had gained because of Eddie's life, Queenie reminded a
crowded church how to love. Through her leadership, the Edward L.
Urbanowski Memorial Fund was established. (For more information
about how to contribute to Eddie's memorial fund, see Appendix B:
Community Opportunities and Resources.)

SKILL BUILDING LESSON

1. Go to Appendix A and complete the self-assessment
    titled "The Adversity in My Life and Leadership."
2. Be willing to ask *What if...*
3. Make a list of the pros and the cons of potential coura-
    geous actions. Which has more weight? Which action is
    the right thing to do, regardless of the consequences?
4. Look for role models who do what you dare to do.
    Observe them. Read about them. Learn from them.
5. When you don't find role models doing what you dare
    to do, do it anyway.
6. Make frequent deposits into your bank of courage. Keep
    a log of brag-able moments for your eyes only. When
    questioning your abilities, review your log.
7. Get good at taking risks so you can learn how to fail.
    Failure teaches you how to succeed.
8. Build your self-esteem to a healthy level where you
    know you can fail without feeling like a failure. If you
    don't believe in you, no one else will.
9. Learn how to accept what you cannot change, change
    what you can, and how to know the difference between
    the two.
10. Check your life's baggage at the door.
11. Forgive your failures. Forgive others' failures.
12. Ask for forgiveness. Believe you are forgiven.
13. Continually seek new opportunities to develop and
    pursue your true passions.
14. Start taking risks. Then take larger risks. Stretch your

risk tolerance!

15. Use what you've got: your reserve is larger than you think!

16. Display subtle reminders of your accomplishments.

> *"Far better it is to dare mighty things,*
> *to win glorious triumphs, even though*
> *checkered by failure, than to take rank*
> *with those poor spirits who*
> *neither enjoy much nor suffer much,*
> *because they live in the gray*
> *twilight that knows not victory nor defeat."*
> *—Theodore Roosevelt*

11

INSIGHT SEVEN:
THE PLUS OF ADAPTABILITY

"Imagination is more important than knowledge.
Knowledge is limited, whereas imagination embraces the entire
world – stimulating progress, giving birth to evolution."
—Albert Einstein

The most sophisticated summarization of adaptability came to me while having a conversation on line with a former graduate school classmate. I enthusiastically discussed my new book project and mentioned my discovery that "adaptability" consistently ranked among the top characteristics of highly motivated individuals, charismatic leaders, and well-adjusted people. She humbly responded, "Oh, the Gumby Phenomenon." In the absence of an intellectual response, I simply blurted, "Huh?" Our conversation continued as the line moved along (we were literally waiting on a line—not at our computers.) My friend continued, "Adaptability is your ability to bend, stretch, squeeze under doors, reach high, go low, and transform your molecular composition into different states—just like Gumby."

ADAPTABILITY DEFINED

Adaptability is the opposite of rigid. It is the ability to adjust to your surroundings and anticipate environmental changes. This proactive approach to your life and leadership allows you to put in place flexible systems or "upgradeable" mechanisms of dealing with change rather than being forced to react. In 540 BC, Heraclites said: "There is nothing permanent except change." Accepting this fact allows you to mentally prepare and reduce the costs of reactionary thinking.

Failure to develop your skills of adaptability negatively impacts your potential for happiness and lowers your *Zing!* potential.

ANTICIPATING CHANGE

In the previous two chapters, I pointed out why many of the competing forces you are required to overcome in your life and leadership are not of your own creation; they just happen. I've also pointed out, however, that you have total control over what you do with what you know, and how you choose to respond. Your ability to adapt (or be Gumby-like) requires you to actively determine what you need to know and how you will consistently obtain relevant and reliable information. You also need to go beyond being aware of potential forces of change to predict the outcomes or influences of those forces.

To illustrate this point, ask yourself: If the room was on fire right now, would I know how to get myself to safety? Most likely, you took notice of the large EXIT signs upon your entrance, or would instinctively remember to "stop, drop, and roll," like you were taught as a child. Whether you realize it or not, you already had a strategy in the event of a fire. You did this out of habit and out of your natural instinct to survive. Do you take this approach in all aspects of your life and leadership?

BENEFITS OF ADAPTING

It's worth repeating; by doing nothing to prepare for your future, you are actually going backwards. Whether you want to adapt isn't the issue. The need for change exists because change exists. You have to adapt and prepare for change; otherwise, you become extinct or risk harmful consequences. Staying alive is the number one reason to learn how to adapt and change with your environment. The number two reason is that you'll be lots more fun. You can't possibly expect to *Zing!* if you become devastated every time a new person is hired, it rains when the forecast said sunny, or your child gets a new girlfriend.

For example, I once gave an entire keynote speech for a state conference in a parking lot standing on a chair. The conference center was experiencing "difficulties" with their air conditioning system. Consequently, the fire alarms consistently went off. At one point, in an attempt to re-wire the air conditioning system, an electrical short occurred causing an actual fire. As I quickly jumped off my chair to let the fire trucks through, I pulled from my "imaginary speaker survival skills handbook" the skill of adaptability and humorously taught the audience how to "stop, drop, and roll!"

CHEESY CHANGE

Adaptability can be broken down to include your ability to think outside the box, manage change, and continually improve your personal skill sets. In Who Moved My Cheese *by Spencer Johnson, two mice and two humans are challenged to make it through the "maze of life" in search of their cube of cheese (i.e. success, happiness, and goal achievement). The humans, of course, exert lots of initial energy and get to their cheese quickly. And, like most humans, they become comfortable, complacent and call it "home." The mice, however, keep their sneakers with them at all times. They keep accessing the amount of cheese left and predict how long it will last. Before it's too late, the mice—not distracted by all the materialistic accumulations the two humans have put in their "home"—move on to find a new source of cheese. Clearly the mice understood the ins and outs of a maze. The mice were willing to leave their zone of comfort and were prepared to consistently move and make adjustments.*

ADAPTABILITY IS A PLUS

The story of the two mice and two men also illustrates the benefits of being adaptable. Adaptability keeps you moving forward, requires you to assimilate information, and necessitates the learning of information normally not of interest. Furthermore, it requires sharpened skill-sets of communication, planning, organization, energy optimization, and creativity, to name a few. Not only does your intellectual capability expand with adaptability, but your reliance on others to "give me the projections" or "tell me where I'm going" also diminishes. Influential individuals figure out their direction by using trustworthy information, a clear understanding of past practices, conversations with reliable sources, and their own deductions. To be truly happy, you need to be truly invested in your future.

THE CONSEQUENCES OF FAILING TO ADAPT

Failure to be adaptable quickly becomes an individual detractor. It lowers your ZQ. People will move on regardless of the time it takes you to "get on board." Show enthusiasm or delight in the mystery of the unknown. Doing so will show others that you are not fearful of change and that you neither doubt your own abilities nor lack the intelligence or skills to accommodate to something new.

Can you notice when you are being told you lack this essential skill of *Zing!*? For example, when someone says to you "I'm not sure you are management material," or "You're not a team player," or "You aren't the type of person who would be interested in …" consider the possibility that you are politely being told: *You're not adaptable.*

THE LOOK OF RIGIDITY

You will come off as rigid or inflexible if you do some, or all, of the following traits:

- Consistently resist or speak against change
- Sabotage those who risk self-improvement by speaking negatively of them
- Complain about any and all new systems, policies, or changes
- Appear disorganized or flustered over minor changes to your schedule
- Consistently look as if you are playing catch-up, paying bills late, or running late
- Rarely subscribe to resources related to advancements in your field or area of interest
- Speak frequently about the "way things used to be"
- Keep bragging about your new 8-Track cassette player

WHY THINGS STAY THE SAME

Over the past twenty years, I have watched the American collegiate social fraternity system struggle with underage drinking, high school sports teams struggle with hazing, and political forces within school districts protect inadequate teachers. Despite the great things all three groups have accomplished, they still can't fix what's broken.

Why? Because people resist change. They either choose to move forward or choose to stay in the past. The Dali Lama said: "There is no present. There is merely the past interfacing with the future." You *Zing!* when your life and leadership become "user friendly" to change and you believe *the future is yours to create*. Consider the following reasons why organizations, for instance, get stuck:

- Frequent leadership turnover without adequate transitional strategies
- Organizational systems prohibit adequate exchange of information
- Inadequate recording mechanisms or archiving
- Lack of value placed on organizational creativity
- False security found in romanticizing tradition for tradition's sake—or tenure
- Goal setting and visionary thinking are not valued
- Lack of needed skill-sets or training for skill-sets
- "Mob mentality" winning over valid individual concerns
- Fear of failing
- Fear of succeeding

HOW TO ANTICIPATE CHANGE

THE SEVEN FORCES OF CHANGE

I knew it was a bad sign when the tech support for Dell started laughing after I asked about buying an extended warranty on my three-year-old laptop! He said it wasn't "worthy of warranty." I became a victim of the rapid pace in which technology influences our lives. To help you predict and prepare for change, consider the following forces that initiate change: Personal; Cultural; Economic; Educational; Political; Geographical; and, Social Forces.

How proficient you are at learning about each force's historical influence will determine how accurately you will be able to predict and prepare for the future. This is a rather pragmatic approach to change prediction. For instance, you know from history that crime rates go up where high school graduate rates are low. You know from history that war in the Middle East causes petroleum prices in the United States to climb, therefore causing air travel to climb, therefore causing… You can predict the future, to some degree, by examining the past.

THE PROCESS OF CHANGE

You can also predict how people will handle transition using a more subjective approach. When faced with the need to change (anticipated, or at your doorstep), our human nature prompts us to be apprehensive, uncomfortable, unpredictable, or excited. You might feel one of these things or a host of other active emotions, including anger, frustration, or cautious optimism. By understanding the predictable set of emotions and responses involved in change, the *Zing!* personality is more likely to jump into change with both feet than be left behind. I believe change occurs in the following five stages:

CHAOS OR "TRUST YOUR GUT" STAGE:

The first stage begins with an internal feeling. Difficulty ensues when you know *instinctively* that it's time to adapt or reinvent yourself or the direction of your company, career, or major, yet others continually resist or disagree. Observe the resistance and chaos around you, but take the lead anyway. Ironically, it's often easier to move on when there isn't a choice. Mandatory isn't always a bad thing.

CLEARING OF ATTITUDES STAGE:

When you realize the reason to change or adapt isn't going away, you finally accept the fact change is going to happen, like it or not. You arrive at a gut level acceptance that it's "change or be changed" time. Now is the time to talk about the benefits of making adjustments, praise others for their cooperation, and clearly keep your eye on the horizon. You stop giving attention to the negativity and focus on those who will help you move forward.

CHANNELING OF ACTIONS STAGE:

With the decision to change behind you, your positive energy now actively moves toward assessing the current state of affairs, determining the nature of the needed change, clarifying the new direction, considering who needs to know what and why, defining the rational, identifying and anticipating the biggest blockers, creating a "change campaign," and making a decision to commit to the new "program." Ripples form.

COMMITMENT STAGE:

In this stage, *you are changing something*. Your actions create energy that fuels more action. It's too late to turn back. Previous resisters may still block your efforts, but their resistance is no longer your concern. Whether or not they admit it, they admire your courage. You have won their favor, yet they may never tell you.

CONFIDENCE STAGE:

In this final stage of change, you clearly have a defined course of action representative of your vision or purpose. You continually adapt and make adjustments without losing sight. Being one of the most noticeable *Zing!* traits, your sense of confidence is drawing people towards your ideas and life. In other words, getting good at change automatically elevates your ZQ!

SKILL BUILDING LESSON

1. Go to Appendix A and complete the self-assessment titled "Then and Now."
2. Buy a Gumby figurine to put on your dashboard or desk.
3. Read adventure books.
4. Walk down the stairs on the left side.
5. Plug person examples into the seven forces of change.
6. Practice writing with your opposite hand for an entire day. Watch how you improve.
7. Require others to call you a different name for an entire week.
8. Use your day-planner to predict who around you will do what and when.
9. When planning for change, clearly articulate your change rationale.
10. Once you clearly define the rationale, define the change.

11. Anticipate obstacles or obstructions before you announce that change is going to happen.
12. Openly discuss the fear(s) of change.
13. Reward yourself (and others) for being adaptable.
14. Keep living plants in your office or home—they only grow if you take care of them!
15. Read *Who Moved my Cheese* by Spencer Johnson.

ANOTHER TACK

By Lilburn Harwood Townsend

"When you suspect you're going wrong,
Or lack the strength to move along
With placid poise among your peers,
Because of haunting doubts or fears:
It's time to for you to shift your pack,
And steer upon another tack!

When wind and waves assail your ship,
And anchors from the bottom slip;
When clouds of mist obscure your sun,
And foaming waters madly run:
It's time for you to change your plan
And make a port while yet you can!

… When Failure opens your luckless door,
And struts across the creaking floor;
When Fortune flees and leaves your air,
And former friends but coldly stare:
It's time for you to take a tack,
And show the world you're coming back!

12

Insight Eight:
The Positives of Attitude

"No pessimist ever discovered the secret of stars,
or sailed to an un-chartered land,
or opened a new doorway for the human spirit."
—Helen Keller

If you've ever gotten up on the wrong side of the bed, then you understand what can happen when you go through the day like The Grouch from *Sesame Street*. Your poor attitude causes predictable reactions by those around you. You provoke negative emotions (i.e. resentment, frustration, anger, distain, etc.) in others. Instead of working with you, people turn against you. And then, in response to *their* behaviors, *you* became further agitated and combative—or withdrawn and unproductive. By the end of the day (and it's been a lousy one) you have no one to blame but the wrong side of your bed. But the wrong side of your bed didn't go to work... you did! You got the day you created.

The Four Kinds of People in the World

I believe four kinds of people live in the world: those who see the glass as half-empty, those who see the glass as half-empty and hate what's left in it, those who see the glass as half-full, and those with *Zing!*. A *Zing!* attitude causes you to notice how much water is in the glass, then inspires you to immediately go in search of a water fountain. Attitude is a powerful thing. Keith Harrell, attitude expert and author of *Attitude is Everything*, writes, "Your attitude dictates whether you are living life or life is living you. Attitude determines whether you are on the way or in the way."

When you arise in the morning, are you aggravated by the hole in the middle of your bagel? If sailing on the ill-fated Titanic, would you have been swearing at the iceberg, or looking for the lifeboat? More importantly, how would those who know you answer these questions on your behalf? Nothing is as transparent as your attitude. You carry it wherever you go for all to see. And nothing is as significant to your potential to *Zing!*.

ZING! ATTITUDE

A positive attitude clearly arises from the desire to be happy and make others happy. A positive attitude communicates all you need to say about your outlook on life and the potential you have to override competing forces to positively impact others towards a greater societal good. A positive attitude is not sugarcoating bad news, offering superficial praise, or giving overly optimistic and unrealistic assessments of situations. It is about your *choice of approach*. You choose your attitude. Of all the things in this world that you cannot control, your attitude is not one of them. Do you engage in behaviors that reflect a positive or negative attitude? Do you know the difference? Positive behaviors increase your ZQ. Negative behaviors are individual detractors. Consider the list of behaviors below. Which do you use more often?

POSITIVE	NEGATIVE
Say "Good morning."	Grunt.
Ask "How can I help?"	Ask "What's in it for me?"
Eat a healthy breakfast.	Consider coffee and two Advil a meal.
Laugh at yourself.	Make fun of others.
Praise.	Criticize.
Work out.	Freak out.
Look to create the future.	Blame your past.
Optimize your energy.	Manage your time.
Ask lots of questions.	Claim to know all the answers.
Speak the truth.	Lie to self-preserve.
Set goals.	Carry your baggage wherever you go.

Speak positively of others.	Spread rumors and gossip.
Have confidence in your abilities.	Have low self-esteem.
Train other leaders.	Need to control others.
Consider yourself replaceable	Sabotage others' advancement.
Say "I'm sorry."	Say "I'm right."
Open doors for others.	Cut in line.
Don't watch the clock.	Count down to 5 pm.
Volunteer.	Watch T.V. or play video games for hours.
Read for pleasure.	Surf the net.
Take additional coursework.	Complain about knowledge acquisition.
Think critically.	React without knowing the facts.
Ask for help.	Fabricate.

FACTORS AFFECTING ATTITUDE

You can change your attitude instantly. Like turning a light switch on and off, you can instantly go from a negative to a positive attitude. You can recognize when your behaviors are individual detractors and immediately replace them with behaviors reflective of who you really want to be. Not only do the people around you deserve this effort, but you deserve it!

THE ROLE OF SELF-ESTEEM

A positive attitude is a direct reflection of your self-esteem. To be more charismatic, you must consistently focus on responsibility and not blame. When you blame, speak negatively of others, and/or remain fearful of taking risks, you are really saying "I'm not worthy." You demonstrate that the only way to build yourself up is to take others down. Similarly, when parents criticize other children's behavior, it is because they are unable to accept the negative behaviors in their own children. Students who mock their professors project their lack of academic preparation. In order to earn respect, you need to own the consequences of your actions.

THE ROLE OF BLAME

When you continually look for a fault rather than a solution, don't be fooled into believing you are deflecting criticism from you onto someone else. You are not made of Teflon. Not only do you lose favor in the eyes of those getting blamed (regardless of whether or not it's their fault), but you could apply your energy to better training of employees, encouraging a different approach or resolution, and building the esteem of your co-workers, as opposed to reinforcing their inadequacies. Playing the blame game on a regular basis diminishes your effectiveness as a leader and sends a clear message to others that they may be the next target of your insecurity.

THE ROLE OF NEGATIVE TALK

Charismatic leaders do not speak negatively of others. It's that simple. They always notice the good in others and they actively verbalize that goodness. I don't buy the "I just need to vent" defense. Never doubt that when someone speaks negatively in your presence about someone else, they will also speak negatively of you in others' presence. Such transparency requires the charismatic leader to refute negative claims and replace them with compliments.

POSITIVES ATTRACT

Negativity attracts negativity. *Zing!* attracts *Zing!*. Negative attitudes make you miserable. Positive attitudes lead to happiness. Remember: The energy you exert is the energy you attract. More specifically, the type of energy you exert is the type of life you'll lead—happy or sad. As you change behaviors to reflect your desire to be happier, others respond in your favor. You begin to create a cycle of positive energy that gains momentum with every positive response created and received.

One of the quickest ways to be positive is to start associating with more positive people. They are the happy ones! They walk quickly down the hallway, as opposed to acting as if every step was at an altitude of twenty thousand feet. Positive people smile and greet you beyond a brief "Hello." Consider the examples below of how to respond when walking past someone you don't know. With each response and action, you communicate an increasingly positive level of *Zing!*.

Verbal Message: "Hello."
Supporting Behavior(s): Nod. Keep on walking.

Verbal Message: "Hello. How are you today?"
Supporting Behavior(s): Smile and brief eye contact. Keep on
   walking.

Verbal Message: "Good morning. How are you on this beautiful day?"
Supporting Behavior(s): Smile, sustained eye contact, and
   hand gesture. Slows down to hear response.

Verbal Message: "Good morning. What brings you here on
   this beautiful day?"
Supporting Behavior(s): Smile, sustained eye contact, and
   handshake. Stops to respond and possibly offers a
   follow-up question, introduction, and/or conversation.

The last exchange clearly demonstrates the intent to make the
other person feel worthy or validated. That's the *Zing!* attitude. If
you are shy, then practice adding actions and words, as suggested
above. I encourage you to be true to your personality; however,
incorporate into your natural style behaviors that will increase your
Zing! Such as: laughter, smiling, eye contact, active listening, walking
with a quick pace, wearing cheerful clothing or a fun tie, hugging,
good posture, and praising.

NEGATIVE SIGNALS
Individual detractors in your *Zing!* Impact Equation are easily
correctable. For example, avoid the following verbal messages in
your greetings:

• Swear words
• Slang expressions
• Speaking after you have passed the individual
• statements lacking in sincerity
• speaking too softly

When greeting someone, avoid these behaviors as well:

- No or little eye contact
- Slouched shoulders
- Slow, dragging pace
- Noticeable change of direction to avoid contact
- Head remains down
- No smile, only words

SKILL BUILDING LESSON

1. Go to Appendix A and complete the self-assessment titled "A Matter of Attitude."
2. Let go of friends who bring you down.
3. Play at work and work at play.
4. Exercise on a regular basis.
5. Learn to say "no."
6. Don't major in the minors.
7. Look for ways to make someone's day.
8. Pay for the person behind you at the toll booth.
9. Sing in the shower.
10. Dance in the streets.
11. Laugh out loud.
12. Give thanks for your day.
13. Spend time alone.
14. Read inspirational books.
15. Use a calendar with inspirational quotes.
16. Send yourself flowers.
17. Plant a garden.
18. Choose happiness.

"Don't be fooled by the deceiver,
when the deceiver is always with you."
—Plato

INSIGHT NINE:
THE MAGNETISM OF PRAISE

"Praise is the heart of kindness."

Wouldn't it be great to get up every morning to a standing ovation? As your feet hit the floor, you hear applause coming from every room, followed by "More! More!" You shower, thinking *I hope there's enough of me to go around today*, and bellowing "I ain't nothin' but a hound dog..." while you scrub. You start your day with a smile on your face. As you leave your house, you shout, "Elvis has left the building!" Your neighbors stand on their front porches with their bic lighters high over their heads and the flames barely noticeable in the blazing sun. You know you rock!

From a standing ovation to a thank-you card, you have many ways to make someone's day and enhance his/her sense of self. You raise your ZQ when you project your positive sense of self onto someone else in the form of praise. When you praise, you willingly give away or actively share your *Zing!*. As a bonus, every gesture of making someone else feel better in your presence makes you feel better in return.

BECAUSE YOU CAN

When in doubt about whether to offer someone praise, think of this quote by management consultant and author Ken Blanchard. He says, "Good thoughts not delivered mean squat." Increase your ZQ by increasing the frequency with which you offer praise. Specifically, never leave a conversation without leaving your partner with a compliment. The last emotion you want another human being to feel in your presence is joy. Compliments create joy.

It takes the human brain 44% longer to register an insult than it does to register a compliment. As social creatures, I attribute this to a natural need to be validated and positively stroked. When receiving an insult, you have to say to yourself "Wait; I think my very being is being questioned." Then, up go the defense mechanisms, rationales, and decisions about how to react, if at all. A compliment, however, is a smile you give to someone's soul.

THE LOOK OF PRAISE

The more creative you are with your praise for someone's effort, appearance, thoughts, existence, and so on, the more meaningful. Expand your definition of praise and increase the odds of reaching more people and having a greater influence. Try using the following four ways to show someone praise. They can be carried out formally and informally.

RECOGNITION

Recognition lets people know that you notice their efforts, ideas, and contributions. Specifically, gratitude is a valuable form of recognition and often grossly underestimated. In *1001 Ways to Reward Employees*, Bob Nelson reports that "studies indicate employees find personal recognition more motivational than money." In other words, managers consistently need to thank employees for a job well done.

Individuals with *Zing!* notice the small things as well as the big things and do not save recognition solely for those in a position to advance their cause. They recognize others because they see others deserving of recognition. Award ceremonies, invitations to dinner, congratulation cards, tipping the hotel maid, giving a day off, a phone call, or dropping by unannounced to articulate your observations, will leave the recipient impressed that you recognized his/her efforts.

ATTENTION

You always want to have 20/20 vision when it comes to observing the world around you (and those in it.) You increase your *Zing!* when you really see other people. Do you ignore some people but pay attention to others? Does one person get a handshake while another gets a dull "Hello?" To *Zing!* is to validate everyone in your presence, as opposed to making them feel unimportant, unappreciated, or undervalued. When you converse with someone and look around the room for someone else to talk to at the same time, you send a very clear message to your conversation partner, "You're not good enough." Treat and greet everyone you meet the same way all the time.

COMPENSATION

In *First, Break All the Rules*, Marcus Buckingham and Curt Coffman do a wonderful job of summarizing specific motivational and environmental working conditions that lead to desirable business outcomes. Using research conducted by the Gallup Organization over the past thirty years, they provide powerful support for looking beyond traditional compensation packages as employees' preferred source of compensation. Instead, they offer thirty-four responses, or "themes," directly correlated to the business outcomes of profitability, customer service, and employee retention.

Supervisors or employers who lack *Zing!* believe "If you pay, they will stay." Not true. Expand your interpretation of compensation to include things like flexible working hours, complimentary refreshment set-up, "extra credit" opportunities, access to special services, occasional complimentary tickets to a show or ball game, information or resources about things of employees' interests, preferred parking spots, priority in office hours, and inviting someone to represent, present, or serve on your behalf. Be creative.

EVALUATION

Evaluation allows you to directly and indirectly facilitate students', teachers', or employees' development while acknowledging their current skill-sets. Evaluation can be such a powerful tool of praise and worth using on a daily basis. How you conduct the evaluation differentiates the charismatic from the controlling, or the personable from the obnoxious. For example, instead of telling a restaurant server who provided you with poor customer service, "I would have left you a bigger tip had you earned it," *Zing!* thinkers would say (followed by leaving a 15% tip), "It looks like you had a considerable amount of tables to handle all at once. Although it would have been nice to see more of you, I'm sure it's been a frustrating evening for you." The end result is constructive versus critical.

When evaluating others, ask yourself "What good can I see in this person?" Look for the good. Point out the good. That's exactly what enjoyable relationships are made of: good intentions backed by productive praise. Saying nothing at all, whether or not you realize it, is often interpreted as negative reinforcement. Err on the side of too much feedback. Bring your *Zing!* to your every thing.

How Strange

Interestingly, praise is often thought to be more genuine if offered by a complete stranger. The recipient takes your compliment at face value because he/she believes you to have no ulterior motive or hidden agenda. What's more, your compliment does not stop with the intended benefactor; when you praise publicly, others may hear or witness the interaction. After you are gone, they see the smile on the recipient's face or the instantaneous change in his/her attitude. Consequently, they too are inspired to praise someone they encounter during their day.

Skill Building Lesson

1. Go to Appendix A and complete the self-assessment titled "Praise Preparation."
2. Be creative with the means you use to praise.
3. Praise in public.
4. Criticize in private.
5. Reduce how often you criticize.
6. Be timely in sending thank-you cards.
7. Send thank-you cards.
8. Avoid saving a reason to give someone attention.
9. Conduct daily evaluations and avoid the stressful "annual review."
10. Look for the good in everyone you meet.
11. Notice something new about someone you see often.
12. Do a better job of saying "please" and "thank-you."

13. Set aside resources for gifts of recognition.
14. Forget about emailing praise and pick up the phone instead.
15. Observe how others show appreciation.
16. Read books on how to recognize and reward employees.
17. Ask those around you how they know someone values them.
18. Go to www.redenvelope.com for recognition ideas.1
19. Keep people "in the loop" as a means of showing you value their efforts.
20. Pay a compliment during every conversation.
21. When angry at someone, praise them instead.

"Brains, like hearts, go where they are appreciated."
—Robert McNamara

14

Insight Ten:
The Rules of Respect

"Tact is the art of seeing people as they wish to be seen."
—Dr. Michael Le Boeuf

I love the "down time" I sometimes get on the road. When I find myself in a hotel room after an evening speech, I take great pleasure in sole possession of the remote control. It's mine. I can watch what I want. The show *Extreme Makeover* is one of my favorites. In front of my very eyes, people transform themselves from frumpy to fabulous. I often wonder, however, if anything other than their exterior has been upgraded.

A Working Definition of Respect

Respect is the ability to hold someone in high regard or esteem. To respect other human beings is to want to give them your best all the time; not because someone (or something) is forcing you; but rather because you sincerely believe they deserve it.

The ability to respect others begins with self-respect. Do you admire your life and leadership? Is it worth admiring? Are you doing what you need to do internally to go from frumpy to fabulous? If you display anything less than self-respect, others will see right through your superficial attempts to show them respect. Said William Hazlitt: "A man meets with no more respect than he exacts." In other words, behave in a manner that reflects a positive sense of self. Take care of your mind, spirit, and body. Avoid being reckless. Be trustworthy, reliable, and honest.

How to Demonstrate Respect

Appearance

One of the most obvious indicators of respect is how you choose to appear in someone's presence. Of course, your appearance should reflect what you are trying to accomplish in a specific environment. But if you want to *Zing!* or impress, then your attire, grooming and overall appearance, needs to be more of a priority than if you are merely looking to hang out with friends or walk your dog.

I chuckle at college students who wear their pajamas to class. They have misinterpreted their learning environment as one of casual or passive learning, as opposed to active engagement with a professor. A collegiate classroom is not a bedroom; it is a place of intellectual exchange. Albeit comfortable, students in pajamas unknowingly project disrespect to their professors. What would students think if all of their professors came to class in their pajamas?

As a general rule, to make a positive impression or maintain a position of influence (even authority) in a specific situation or environment, use the "plus one" rule of appearance. For example, when I walk into a room where I'll be speaking, other people should be able to conclude from my appearance (and behavior) that I am the speaker. Prior to the speaking date, I inquire as to what the audience will be wearing, then dress slightly more formal. I do this out of respect for my audience.

The more casual you dress, the harder it is for others to determine your role, and the greater the assumption (by others) that you might not be taking your role seriously. Appearance is a touchy subject. I know substance matters. I also know that clothes do not make the man—or woman. However, if you combine respectful behaviors with appropriate appearance you will reap the benefits of *Zing!*.

Method of communication

You also demonstrate respect for others by how you choose to communicate. Not only does your word selection have the potential to *Zing!*, but the noise level of your conversation also matters. As a parent, I empathize with the frustration of parenting. As an educator, I empathize with children who have been made to feel worthless by teachers who, instead of speaking, merely yell at them. As difficult as it may be, if you seriously want to improve your capacity to demonstrate respect, you must speak to others—especially children—with respect. This means avoiding sarcasm, mimicking a speech pattern, or mockingly mouthing words. It also means refraining from raising your voice out of anger, frustration, or disappointment (unless it's a matter of someone's safety). No one likes to be yelled at. Respect others by avoiding the temptation to intimidate, oppress, frighten, degrade, or control. When you do this, *you* are the one out of control. Work less on volume and more on content. (For example, instead of yelling at your kids, put yourself in a "time out!")

WORD SELECTION AND GESTURES

Word selection and the content of your statements can also quickly show someone that either you respect them or you have no regard for their values, morals, and diversity. For example, the use of profanity, stereotyping, racist remarks, sexist jokes, and slang in your conversations may be an integral part of your culture, but shows little appreciation for those not familiar with or part of that culture. Likewise, obscene gestures, winking, slapping someone on the butt, etc. to communicate, may be perceived as offensive and oppressive and are big individual detractors. No doubt about it; leave these out.

PUNCTUALITY

The venues or events you attend, and the time you arrive at those venues, demonstrate the level of respect you have for the planners and those in attendance. Perpetual lateness is another significant (and preventable) individual detractor that subjects itself to a variety of interpretations and/or assumptions about you as: disorganized, rude, careless, inconsiderate, or having other priorities. A friend told me that her boss instilled the importance of punctuality with this saying, "'Early' is 'on time' and 'on time' is 'late'!" *Zing!* requires you to be on time. Stop apologizing and put post-its around your house or office to remind you of appointments. Avoid over-scheduling.

Moreover, your ability to prioritize someone else's time (and manage your own time) directly signals their importance to you. Whose time is more important? For example, you may arrive on time, but if you leave early, you have done the same thing as if you had arrived late. It is far better to re-schedule than ignore the fact that someone else, or a group of individuals, made time for you but you did not reciprocate. Cutting a speech short because you have to catch a plane, not eating at a lunch meeting because you have another lunch engagement, or sitting down for coffee without taking off your coat are all subtle signs of disrespect.

Did you realize that with every missed dinner, weekend trip to the office, and failure to show up to your child's recital, you send the message: "You are only worthy of my left-over time"? To respect your family is to be there when you say you'll be there. Honor them with your presence. The same applies to friendships, volunteer commitments, and so on. Bosses who call employees on Easter Sunday, for example, show complete disrespect for their employees' family time. Bosses who call employees all hours of the day and night show complete self-absorption. Power does not grant you respect any more than a title or position makes you a leader.

INVOLVEMENT

Another very important way of showing respect is by your level of involvement in your workplace or community. For example, you can attend a Little League game coached by your colleague. You can volunteer to chaperone your son's class field trip. When I speak at my local library, my friends all show up—and sit in the front row! Their support is a sign of their respect. Although they've heard me speak many times, they still participate, ask questions, and laugh at my jokes. What can you attend or do to show the people you know (or work for) that you respect them?

Respect is also demonstrated by inviting others' opinions and participation. Sometimes the kindest words you can say are: "Can I bounce an idea off of you?" What the recipient hears is: *You have a brain in your head and I respect your take on this.* Have you ever been asked to serve on a committee because someone respects your talents? It's flattering to be invited to do more work! Supervisors who micro-manage show very little trust (and thus, respect) for their employees' abilities. What they project on a daily basis is: *You can do this, but I want to check it.* To dignify others' talents, opinions, and ideas is to encourage their presence, involvement, and participation in the decision-making process. Who would be honored to work with you?

EXPECTATIONS

Connected to the notion of inviting others' ideas and participation is the holding of high expectations for *their* life and leadership. Warren Bennis (a man I highly respect) says, "Great expectations are evidence of great respect." In other words, by letting others know your expectations of/for them, you are telling them how you perceive them. Just as high expectations demonstrate high esteem, low expectations demonstrate low esteem. When you undervalue, underpay, and under-appreciate your workers, you simply disrespect them. When you prevent access, limit upward mobility and promotion, or assume a lack of interest in their lives, you simply disrespect them.

POLITENESS

Politeness is one of the best ways to demonstrate your respect for others as well as for yourself. Politeness may require little more than a spoken "please" and "thank-you."

IN A NUTSHELL

Ultimately, your goal is to put your need for immediate gratification or self-importance behind that of others. Show others the proper respect and your ZQ increases. Your self-respect also increases. Whether your family, co-workers, employees, neighbors, etc., deserve your respect isn't the issue; your number one goal is to act on the belief that you are not the center of the universe.

SKILL BUILDING LESSON

1. Go to Appendix A and complete the self-assessment titled "RESPECT."
2. Respect yourself.
3. Establish relationships with people you respect. Observe how they treat others.
4. Follow through on your promises.
5. Arrive 15 minutes early for all appointments.
6. Return phone calls within 24 hours.

7.   Stand up quickly upon seeing someone approach you.
8.   Stand when shaking someone's hand.
9.   Give your seat to someone else who needs it more than you do (i.e. the elderly, a child).
10. Ask someone how he or she would like to be addressed before addressing him or her. Use someone's formal name (i.e. Mrs. Jones) unless instructed otherwise.
11. When someone else is speaking, listen without interruption.
12. Hang up your phone—or refrain from taking a call—if in a conversation with someone else.
13. Turn off your cell phone before a conversation or at a public venue.
14. Cover your mouth if you yawn.
15. Slow down before approaching a door to let others go ahead of you.
16. Hold a door open for someone.
17. Refrain from putting your seat back on a plane without first asking permission from the person behind you.
18. Offer food or drink to others before you take one.
19. Wait until everyone has been served before eating.
20. If someone drops something, quickly pick it up for them.
21. Buy and read an etiquette book.

> *"If I hold my expectations high enough you will strive to achieve them. If I keep them low enough, you will certainly meet them."*

15

INSIGHT ELEVEN:
THE NECESSITY OF NOURISHMENT

"Faith keeps the person that keeps the faith."
—*Mother Teresa*

I sometimes think there just aren't enough boxes of *Wheaties* cereal to go around. Although the cereal is tasty (and a wonderful source of dietary fiber) it's the outside of the box that gets my attention. Since 1924, *Wheaties* has been the official "breakfast of champions," honoring "inspirational role models and champions in their community through their charitable endeavors." The first athlete to grace the box cover was Lou Gherig in 1934. Since then, Bob Richards (1958), Chris Evert (1987), Tiger Woods (1998), and Lance Armstrong (1999) are among those who have proudly met the criteria for becoming a "cover model." Etched in my mind forever is the 1977 *Wheaties* box cover with Bruce Jenner in his red, white, and blue track uniform. Every time I think of this box cover, I am inspired. This image epitomizes success for me. It represents the results of years of physical training, mental toughness, extraordinary conditioning, and proper nourishment. Of course, these things lead to much more than the cover of a cereal box.

HAVING WHAT IT TAKES

Do you have the energy you need to optimally perform in your life and leadership? *Zing!* requires energy. The ability to exert and sustain positive energy, for instance, is something only *you* can do for you. Fundamental to your ability to do anything else for anyone else is your health and wellness.

In *The Power of Full Engagement*, Jim Loehr and Tony Schwartz note: "Great leaders are stewards of organizational energy. They begin by effectively managing their own energy. As leaders, they must mobilize, focus, invest, channel, renew and expand the energy of others." If you are perpetually exhausted by the daily demands on your time, consistently ill, or have difficulty coping with stress, you simply don't have enough energy to fuel your own needs, let alone anyone else's needs.

FEED ME! FEED ME!

The four sources of nourishment for your life and leadership can be categorized as physical, emotional (or psychological), spiritual, and intellectual (or mental). The benefits of nourishing all four sources of energy (as opposed to only focusing on one or two) are numerous because of the continual interfacing among them. For example, there will be times when the demands on your body leave you not only physically exhausted but emotionally spent. Your tired body will cause you to become irritable, cranky, and lethargic. Likewise, when you find yourself frustrated over your inability to generate new ideas, or are emotionally exhausted, you will need to rely on physical movement to re-energize your thinking. The foot bone is connected to the leg bone!

PHYSICAL CONDITIONING AND CARE

Taking care of your body speaks volumes about your sense of self. When you take the time to prioritize your health and fitness, you make a noticeable statement about your self-esteem and self-worth. As a result of a regular exercise regime, your ability to resist disease increases while your blood pressure and cholesterol levels decrease, your circulatory system works more efficiently, you release healthier chemicals in your system, and you reduce the harmful effects of environmental stressors on your body while improving your mood.

THE ROLE OF EXERCISE

Exercise is clearly one of the best ways to take care of your mind and body. Maximize your workouts by alternating the kind of exercise you get every week. Most fitness experts recommend you include a weekly regime of weight lifting, aerobic workouts and interval training. If you don't have a regular workout regime, start now! Exercise (especially when it is your first morning activity) kick starts your metabolism for the entire day. Throughout the day, you continue to benefit from this efficient state of metabolism—or energy creation—and use.

As recognized experts on energy efficiency, Loehr and Schwartz note: "Because energy diminishes both with overuse and with underuse, we must balance energy expenditure with intermittent energy renewal." Therefore, not only is exercise important, but so is rest. To function optimally, you need seven to eight hours of sleep per night. Additional ways to rest is to take breaks during your busy day, alternate tasks, or stop what you're doing, stretch, change your environment or activity, then return.

IT'S THE LAW!

Another way of taking care of your body is to not put it in harm's way. Preventative measures such as wearing a seatbelt, good oral hygiene, not driving while you are tired, and having an annual physical, demonstrate the value you place on good health. Likewise, smoking, binge drinking, drugs, and irresponsible sexual activity can lead to bodily damage, illness, and chronic health problems. *Zing!* requires others to have confidence in your judgment. This includes personal judgment. Think of the last time you saw someone speed by you doing 100 miles an hour and thought, *Wow, how cool is that?* In truth, weren't you hoping they wouldn't end up in an accident?

HEALTHY EATING

Taking care of your body also means watching what you put into your body. Proper diet plays an enormous role in the way glucose (your body's fundamental energy source) is used in your body. Despite the preponderance of diet theories, food fads, and proposed changes to the Food Pyramid, the most reliable course of good nutrition is to eat in moderation, reduce the amount of unrefined sugars and carbohydrates you consume, increase your water consumption to 8 glasses a day (sixty-four ounces), take a daily vitamin and continue to eat a balanced diet of the right protein, fruits, and vegetables. Eating smaller portions more frequently prevents over consumption at one meal. Limiting your caffeine intake is also important to enhanced energy or *Zing!*.

One of the best ways of ensuring your daily endurance is to fuel your body in the morning. Skipping meals (especially breakfast) is like expecting to drive a car a long distance without putting any gas in it. When you skip breakfast, you start your day by running on "fumes." Eat breakfast and take the time to begin every day on the right foot. Not only will this practice give you energy, it will help you to protect against stress.

GOOD AND BAD STRESS

The ill effects of stress on your body are well documented. Like charisma, stress is in the eye of the beholder. Most people are not disturbed by events themselves; but rather by their opinion or perception of those events. Dr. Wayne Dyer says, "Change the way you look at things, and the things you look at change." You have to "see" an event as stressful for it to have a negative psychological effect on your system. Cumulative effects of stress are so often masked, and/or have become so socially acceptable, they are ignored as significant warning signs. Frequent headaches, jaw clinching, gastro-intestinal discomfort, teeth grinding and disruption in sleep patterns, for instance, are the result of your body losing the fight with your head.

Stress doesn't go away; it hides. You must find a way to effectively manage and reduce the harmful effects of stress on your health. Remind yourself "Don't sweat the small stuff," and "It's all small stuff" when the need for perspective arises. Effective means of managing your stress also include daily exercise, proper diet, relaxation techniques, counseling, meditation, proper sleep and elimination of the stressors.

EMOTIONAL AND MENTAL HEALTH

How you handle your feelings affects whether others will view you as capable or in over your head; optimistic or pessimistic; irrational or rational; and so on. Patience, self-control, empathy, joy, happiness, and gregariousness, are emotions that earn others' positive regard.

The ability to consciously recognize which emotions you are displaying is important to any communication's effectiveness. People read emotions before they believe the words being spoken. The tone of your voice, rate of your speech, degree of eye-contact, and nonverbal messages accurately articulate your true feelings. *Zing!* happens when your words match your emotions.

SPIRITUAL HEALTH

Faith is such a vital component in your happiness. Despite the fact that much of the research I conducted for this book views "spirit" to mean your "inner child" or "sense of adventurousness," I use the term as a source of energy derived from your religious beliefs. For example, as a Christian, I believe my spirit reflects my ability to allow a Greater Being warm me from the inside out. We are not alone in this world. Seek a source of internal faith and be open to experience its benefits (i.e. internal peace, comfort, and strength). Jimmy Carter, Mother Teresa, H. H. The Dali Lama, and Martin Luther King, Jr. all possess(ed) strong spirits derived from their religious beliefs. A strong spiritual energy source allows you to step back and view your life and leadership as it relates to a much larger universe. John C. Maxwell in *The 21 Irrefutable Laws of Leadership* says, "People cannot give to others what they themselves do not possess."

INTELLECTUAL HEALTH

Use it or lose it! Research has found that the more we challenge our brain and stretch it to greater intellectual pursuits, the more we increase our capacity to retain knowledge, assimilate ideas, and recall facts. Loehr and Schwartz point out the additional benefit of mental exercise: "Continuing to challenge your brain serves as a protection against age-related mental decline. The key supportive mental muscles include mental preparation, visualization, positive self-talk, effective time management and creativity." Intellectual stimulation and longevity is well documented, yet we often opt for evening television instead of quiet reading. Turn off the tube and pick up a book! You must use these muscles or else you will lose these muscles. When was the last time you were impressed by someone who bragged about being stupid or made the statement: "I haven't read a book in over five years?"

Going and Going, or Fading Fast?

I have often been compared to the Energizer Bunny. I'm not sure this is a compliment, but given my high self-esteem, I take it as such. I'd much rather have too much energy than not enough. What about you? Given the enormous impact of physical, emotional, psychological, and spiritual nourishment on your ZQ, are you willing to do what you need to do to increase that potential (or do you like beige)?

Skill Building Lesson

1. Go to Appendix A and complete the self-assessment titled "Fit to Live and Fit to Lead."
2. Meditate. Take time for self-reflection. Spending time in contemplation is often a wonderful way to prepare for a busy day and anticipate the challenges you will face. Consider the same location every day and at the same time. Pick a peaceful place that allows solitude.
3. Write down your thoughts. Keeping a journal safely allows your most intimate struggles to come to the surface while providing an opportunity to find solutions to problems and release stress.
4. Eat for energy. Go with unprocessed foods whenever possible, bright-colored vegetables, and a limited amount of refined sugars and carbohydrates.
5. Adapt a daily exercise regime. Alternate the types of aerobic workouts from walking to swimming to keep it interesting. Include stretching exercises three times a week and light weight lifting two times a week. Your body is yours for life!
6. Get organized. Manage your stress by optimizing your time and how/where you spend it.
7. Take a proactive approach to scheduling and delegating.

8. Use a To Do list on a daily basis and revise your list every night.
9. Learn to say "no" to over-scheduling your time.
10. Listen to music. Soft, background music calms you. Ocean sounds or falling rain are relaxing.
11. Hug more! Studies consistently show the enormous health benefits resulting from physical touch.
12. Surround yourself with inspirational materials.
13. Read for fun. Go back to school. As noted previously, "garbage in—garbage out!"
14. Subscribe to a magazine, or pick up the latest bestseller.
15. Join a professional association related to your job, community involvement, or hobby.
16. Get a personal trainer or committed friend or colleague to "jump" into a fitness routine with you. If not now, when are you going to get into shape?
17. Get out your calendar and schedule annual medical exams. Which part(s) of your body have you neglected?

"He maketh me lie down in green pastures: he leadeth
me beside still waters."
—Psalm 23:2 (kjv)

16

INSIGHT TWELVE:
THE DRAW OF INTELLIGENCE

"A moment's insight is sometimes worth a life's experience."
—*Oliver Wendell Holmes*

How far would you follow someone who knows less than you know? What do you think about people who think way too much about way too little? The value you place on intelligence will be just as important as your applied intelligence. As you strive to use your IQ, the impact on your ZQ is all positive. People will find you interesting if you have genuine interests. People will seek your opinions when they are pased upon accurate information. When you care about things that cause or effect the past, present, and future, you demonstrate a unique understanding of your place in the world.

Pursuit of knowledge occurs because you value truth. Arguing a position on the basis of personal experience or limited knowledge can often make you look ignorant. The less open you are to conflicting opinions, the more clearly you send the message: I know only what I know.

WHAT IS INTELLIGENCE?

Intelligence is the capacity to acquire information, critically think, employ creativity, compare and contrast information, apply knowledge, use common sense, love learning, incorporate humor and wit, teach, and understand the difference between wisdom and ignorance. The most important of these components is a love of learning. You will always inspire others to do great things if you can demonstrate your continued *desire to learn* great things.

GET THE FACTS

Having parents who were college professors put a damper on my youthful desires to use slang and improper grammar. At the dinner table, my sisters and I were expected to join the conversation, share our opinions, and debate ideas. Regardless of our age, we were reminded of the importance of facts. My mother used to say, "Without facts, how do you know that what you know is worth knowing?" This upbringing taught me something very important and useful throughout my lifetime: knowledge is the foundation of thought. Seek legitimate sources of information from which to draw your conclusions.

SEEK DIFFERENT POINTS OF VIEW

Once you have information, data, and facts, how can you arrange and interpret them in their proper perspective and from different points of view? Perspective is often found in history; you must look at more than the present. Points of view are not found in one opinion; you must seek many opinions. *Zing!* thinkers are sponges who actively pursue a variety of water sources. They remain be open to numerous opinions. Be secure enough in yourself to welcome dissention. Be willing to table votes if there is unanimous agreement because you value (and seek) diverse opinions.

TEACH SOMEONE

I am a fan of any kind of education. The very reason I wrote this book is to inspire those who can read it to help those who can't read it. Teaching someone to read requires knowledge and personal time. Do you have time? Mahatma Gandhi said: "We must be the change we wish to see in this world." He used the verb "be" as an expression of action and ownership. Did it occur to you that your intelligence can make all the difference in the world—literally? If you teach one person to read, then you've changed his/her life forever.

ASK QUESTIONS

There is no such thing as a bad question. Asking questions indicates your desire to collect as much information as you can to make informed decisions, formulate an opinion, and consider various points of views. When you ask questions, you let others know that you value their opinion. Be confident and have courage to ask questions when you don't understand something. Children understand this instinctively. They raise their hand to get the attention of their teacher. When these same children become high school students, they don't want the attention of someone who could help clarify, explain, or direct. Down go their hands. What's changed? It takes *Zing!* to seek others' counsel—and consider it. Always ask questions in a respectful manner, thus leaving the other person's basic human rights intact. Intimidation, threat, and coercion are individual detractors and manipulative means of inquiry.

ADDITIONAL TRAITS OF INTELLIGENCE

Would your coworkers or your peers consider you smart? On what basis would they draw their conclusions? Consider the signals of intelligence below that assess and/or determine your pursuit of knowledge—and the outcome of your pursuit.

The books you read. Can you discuss Dan Brown's *The DeVinci Code* with someone you've just met? Have you read any/all of the *Harry Potter* series? The top ten bestsellers are great conversation starters and demonstrate your love of reading. Which genres interest you—Fiction? Non-fiction? Mystery? Science Fiction? How-to books?

The content of your conversations (including your vocabulary). In other words, what you talk about—and with whom—can greatly increase or decrease your *Zing!*. For example, racist, sexist, vulgar profanity, and discriminatory comments are blatant signs of ignorance, not intelligence. Show a command of the English language, proper grammar, and an extensive vocabulary.

The media to which you expose yourself. You are what you watch and read. Reading offensive materials will project that you are offensive. When you listen to public radio, you project that you value divergent thinking and world views.

Your associations (or lack of) with other intelligent individuals. Who you choose to call friends, colleagues, and associates will reflect upon you. Seek those who know more than you do and befriend them. Be quiet when they speak.

Reference to world affairs. You have to know about the world to know how you will make it a better place. Talk about politics, world economies, and ideologies. Discussions don't have to be solely based upon your opinion, but they can be lively when you share them.

Your ability to grasp new ideas. The speed with which you pick up on new material, thoughts, and ideas suggest your "sharpness."

The level of your participation in conversations. Even if you are shy, try stepping out of your comfort zone and force yourself to make a verbal contribution to conversations. On the other hand, if you tend to dominate conversations you will detract from your ZQ because others will think you don't care about giving them a chance to talk.

Conduct in classes, meetings, or at events. Talking or interrupting while others are talking is rude and suggests your own self-importance or immaturity. Honor your company by paying attention while they are speaking.

Your ability to recall facts and events. When I was in college, John Dean came to speak about Watergate. I was fascinated by his ability to recollect very specific information and conversations with others. To this day, it wasn't just the content of what he said that impressed me, but rather his ability to remember the details.

Appreciation of the arts. A clear sign of your appreciation for history and culture is your appreciation of the theatre, music, and art. These things represent a common bond among humanity. When you take advantage of the opportunities to enrich your cultural experience, you make a statement about your desire to pursue different subjects and become more enlightened, interesting, and well-rounded.

LASTING QUESTIONS

Isn't it easy to forget about the hungry when you eat more than enough every day? Isn't it easy to ignore the homeless when you sleep under a roof every night? Isn't it easy to not hear the cries of abused children when your own children are laughing loudly? Intelligence is much more that what you know, it's what you do about what others fail to do or don't know how to do.

ONE PERSON MAKING A DIFFERENCE

I recently met a man studying and talking to himself in an airport.

"Excuse me. It's been a while since I've seen such interest in a topic. What are you studying?" I asked.

He replied, "Child advocacy laws."

"Are you an attorney?"

He smiled and said, "I wish." He explained (as his ZQ soared...) that he volunteers for CASA and was trying to learn what he needed to know to best serve the child to whom he'd been assigned.[1] At the end of the conversation, he gave me his business card. I discovered, he was the international vice-president for a billion-dollar telecommunications company! He made time to learn about a cause and make a difference.

Remember: Intelligence is like money. It doesn't matter how much you have, but what you do with what you've got! Be smart about your life and leadership. Make it count.

SKILL BUILDING LESSON

1. Go to Appendix A and complete the self-assessment titled "In My Mind."
2. Refrain from discussing how much you don't know about a topic (i.e. I don't know the first thing about Senator Kerry's congressional voting record) reframe your comment to reflect a desire to learn more (i.e. The political process has always fascinated me. It would be interesting to review Kerry's congressional voting record.)

3. Maintain an open mind. One of the quickest ways to be ignorant is to proclaim yourself all knowing! Validate other people's intelligence.
4. Admit when you don't understand something.
5. Read. Read. Read.
6. Learn another language. (After you've begun the process, treat yourself to a vacation in that country!)
7. Pick a figure or event from history and learn all there is to know.
8. Keep in mind, politics don't have to be personal. When first meeting people, withholding your personal political views gives them a chance to be comfortable in your presence.
9. Go back to school. Literally. Many outlets for formal and informal teaching and learning exist. Every school district my children have attended suffers from a vast shortage of substitute teachers. (While substitute-teaching second graders, I learned all about "palindromes." While substitute-teaching sixth graders, I learned about "point of view." While substitute-teaching high school students, I learned to stick with the elementary students...)
10. Get a certificate, degree, another degree or audit a course.
11. Build your vocabulary.
12. Learn about and support a cause.

"The only thing more expensive than education is ignorance."
—Benjamin Franklin

17

INSIGHT THIRTEEN: THE EXAMPLE SETTING OF DETERMINATION

*"Great people are just ordinary people with an
extraordinary amount of determination."*
—Garner Dunkerly, Sr.

It's a bird. It's a plane. No, it's Superman.

I will never look at Superman the same since Christopher Reeve's horse riding accident which left him physically challenged. He may not be able physically to leap tall buildings in a single bound as his character once did; but, the actor believes that hard work and faith will restore the use of his legs. In addition to restoring his physical abilities, Christopher Reeve is equally determined to raise awareness about spinal cord injury patients' needs, increase government financial support, and advance medical research efforts. For many (including me), Superman is not someone in a blue suit with a cape and big "S" on his chest; he is a real man in a real wheelchair with a big "D" for determination on his heart.

DETERMINATION DEFINED

Determination is a sense of certainty, strength, and direction. It reflects your ability to make a decision and act accordingly. To have determination is to be void of uncertainty, "flip flopping," indecision, and/or circumstance. At times, determination has the same charismatic outcome as a clearly articulated vision or purpose; it not only fuels the means to an end, but is a desired attitude in and of itself. The great thing about determination is that you don't always need to know exactly_where_you are going or exactly_how you will get there. If you can communicate an unyielding belief or confidence in your abilities to move forward, then others will have faith in your potential. If you've ever commented about someone, "That person is going places," then you understand determination.

THE BIG MO

Think of those you know personally who you describe as "determined." Now, consider where they started out and where they ended up. Determination is the drive that got them from point A to point B. It is a force greater than opposing forces. It creates momentum and keeps your life and leadership moving forward. Leadership without momentum is like sailing without wind. You can blow into your mainsail (I have personally tested this theory) all day, but you're still not going anywhere because it's just not enough air. Like sailing, once you begin to move—or influence—others toward a desired destination, you begin a process that sustains itself with less energy than it took for you to stand still.

THE LOOK OF DETERMINATION

Characteristics of determined individuals include the ability to stay on task, or focus. You literally say "No!" to distraction and stay your course. You get up after you get knocked down. You take advantage of opportunities to achieve your goals and actively create opportunities. To be determined is to believe in yourself and your basic human rights. You are worthy of achieving happiness. You act on this internal self-esteem. Despite the risks, obstacles, and limited resources, determined individuals accept that if they want something, they have to get it! Hard work pays off. Others may appear to have more advantages or unlimited resources than you, but your belief in the possibility of getting (or becoming) what you want will allow you to achieve your goals and make a difference in the world.

VOCABULARY OF WANTING

Determination requires you to ask for what you want with clear, distinctive language while refusing to apologize for wanting people to follow your lead or assist you. To be determined is to believe in your capabilities and potential. For example, statements like "I need you to…" or "It is important that you…" are more effective than, "If it's not too much of an inconvenience…" or "I know this may be an imposition, but…" Statements like "Here's what I'm going to do…" versus "Someday, I'd like to…" suggests your affirmative direction. Saying "I will do what it takes to…" versus "I'll see where the chips may fall…" suggests that you control your destiny. Practice being decisive and determined in your speech. Respect others' basic human rights, including their right to say "No" to you.

THE THREE D'S OF DETERMINATION

DESTINY

The components of determination are destiny, diligence, and decisiveness. The first component is destiny. Charismatic individuals own their decisions, accept their failures, and refrain from blaming others or list reasons why something didn't go their way. If you have given up on getting what you want or deserve, settle for less, or take the easy way out, then you are admitting defeat—the opposite of determination.

DILIGENCE

The second component of determination is diligence. Diligence is a stick-to-it approach to life and leadership. When you least feel like doing a particular task, sometimes the only thing that sustains you is the heartfelt, "don't give up!" emotion. Anyone who has ever accomplished anything has done so with diligence. In fact, many of my associates in higher education who earned their doctoral degrees often comment that doing so tested their diligence more than anything else!

DECISIVENESS

Decisiveness is the last component to determination. If you've ever looked at someone and said, "Make a decision already!" then you understand the frustration of watching others do nothing because they have too many choices. Individuals with *Zing!* trim their sails along the way because they know that being in motion is better than stalling out. Be willing to risk doing something wrong over doing nothing at all. The next time you are indecisive, ask yourself: What's the worst thing that could happen?_

In *The Contrarian's Guide to Leadership*, Steven B. Samples offers the point of view of doing nothing as the possible right course of action. The contrarian leader's approach to decision- making is to: "Never make a decision yourself that can reasonably be delegated to a lieutenant and never make a decision today than can reasonably be put off until tomorrow." In other words, carefully consider not acting as an option as opposed to not acting out of fear or procrastination.

SOMETHING TO DECIDE

In his bestseller Awaken The Giant Within, *Anthony Robbins tells a story of his early desire to be a public speaker. Making the point about determination, he remembers hearing many bad speakers who, despite their lack of skill, were still getting hired. He realized that if he was any good, he could become quite successful. He also realized that the best way to become a great speaker was to practice. To this end, he set a goal of speaking once a month. Then, he deduced that if he spoke once a week, by the end of the year he would have had 52 opportunities to practice, instead of only 12 opportunities. This still wasn't enough. So, he re-thought his approach and decided to speak twice a week, making almost 104 opportunities to improve his skills and build exposure. Anthony Robbins become one of the country's top speakers in a shorter amount of time through a clear sense of destiny, good decision-making, and diligence (it took many "no, thank-yous" to book that many appearances).*

SKILL BUILDING LESSON

1. Go to Appendix A and complete the self-assessment titled "Determined."
2. Set goals with timelines and deadlines.
3. Break goals down into objectives.
4. Tell others about your goals. Ask or invite others to support your vision—they might be able to connect you with someone who can be a valuable resource.
5. Ask out loud: What's the worst thing that can happen?
6. Decide to change something that needs to be changed.

7. Be direct in your language.
8. Exert a consistent energy to make your vision a reality.
9. Seek mentors who have accomplished what you desire to accomplish.
10. Work around (or ignore, if needed) those who create obstacles.
11. Reward yourself for all accomplishments—small or large.
12. Examine your priorities and eliminate time spent on things that don't matter.
13. Simplify and focus.
14. Replace the words "I don't know what to do," with "I'm going to give it a try."
15. Remember that you do not have to ask for permission to be happy.

"Success seems to be largely a matter of hanging on after others have let go."
—William Feather

18

Insight Fourteen: The Art of Interpersonal Communication

"Person to person. Touch to touch. Face to face.
Hand to hand. Heart to heart. Soul to soul. Eye to eye.
These are the true mediums of human communication.
Everything else is just a technological accomplishment
— an interfacing of our intellects."

I can't dance. Despite this fact, when Al Green starts to sing, I dance. Much to my daughter's embarrassment, I can't help myself. I love to dance. My husband can't dance either. He hides this reality by dancing what he calls the "yard-and-home-maintenance" dances. They fall somewhere between stepping and standing still. Maybe you've seen the "lawn mower" or "hedge clipper" dances? How about the "paintbrush" or "water sprinkler" dances? Much to my embarrassment, he can't help himself either! I completely understand why people tape over their wedding videos.

Walk with me and talk with me. Invite me to dance.

Your ability to express your ideas, articulate your goals, ask for what you want, and challenge others' assumptions requires you to carry your communication skills with you at all times. Effective communication is essential for building healthy relationships, challenging others' development, protecting basic human rights, enacting change, relating on higher levels, getting what you want, and giving others what they need. It is one of the most significant skills you need to *Zing!*.

THE PROCESS OF COMMUNICATION

ONE-WAY

The basic elements of communication include a sender, receiver, message, and feedback. One-way communication occurs when one person sends a message to a receiver in the absence of feedback. Examples include sending an email, giving a lecture, posting a sign, and writing an article. With one-way communication, you never really know if what you sent was received as intended. One-way communication is prone to misinterpretation and misunderstanding. It is often equitable to mass-marketing where "one size fits all."

TWO-WAY

Two-way communication has a feedback loop that enables the receiver to respond to your message and gives you the opportunity to check for his/her comprehension. Examples include personal conversations, instant messaging, and phone conversations. Obviously, when you are face to face with someone, you increase the potential target areas of accurate listening (discussed in the next chapter). For a communication to be considered two-way, an active exchange and feedback must take place. Although now standard practice, email is not two-way communication. Picking up the phone is significantly more engaging than sending someone an email.

The significance of recognizing the type of communication in which you are engaged helps you focus your energies of influence. One-way communication is most appropriate when the receiver's opinion or response is not needed or requested. For example, you praise, honor, celebrate, recognize, lecture, or inform. The other party (or parties') value is not jeopardized because the message is appropriate to the medium. When you want to respect someone's opinion, show regard by bringing someone into the process, or enter into a helping exchange, use two-way communication.

CONSIDERATIONS FOR EFFECTIVE EXCHANGES

PRACTICE AND PREPARE

A high ZQ requires high skills of communication. Broaden how you approach the process. Unlearn skills contrary to your charismatic mission and replace them with more useful ones. If you are overly aggressive, for instance, you can learn to tone down your forcefulness by consciously considering (before you speak) ways to achieve your goal without violating the other person's basic human rights. In another instance, if you are uncomfortable in social settings, you can prepare a strategy for "working the room" before you step foot in the room. As Susan RoAne in her national bestseller *How To Work a Room* notes, "you can learn to overcome many of the roadblocks or obstacles preventing you from talking to strangers." Like any skill, the more you practice, the more you improve. (As a speaker, I practice my remarks in front of a mirror many times before I go onto stage.)

FOCUS ON YOUR SKILLS

The second consideration for effective communication is to worry less about others' skills and more about your own skills. Take responsibility for setting the dance floor, or stage, for better exchanges. For example, make strangers feel comfortable in your presence by using humor. Avoid criticizing the receiver's lack of assertiveness, inappropriate humor, or poor eye contact. This will not make you more charismatic—just the opposite. Attend to your body posturing, sense of space, and actions that might contribute to or cause others' reactions. Before you criticize someone, know their story. Remember, speaking negatively of others is an individual detractor.

ONE SIZE DOESN'T FIT ALL

Lastly, know that there are many different types of communication skills. Just because you are proficient at one or two doesn't mean you are proficient at all of them. For instance, speakers who write are often accused (by editors) of writing like we speak! We are good at oral communication, but not necessarily at expressing ourselves on paper. Knowing this information is helpful because it encourages speakers who write to hire good editors. What are your communication strengths and weaknesses?

THE SKILLS OF COMMUNICATION

Skills used to exchange information and communicate include: rhetoric, public speaking (Chapter 20), written expression, mediation, paraphrasing, counseling, listening (Chapter 19), assertiveness, confrontation, documentation and research, conflict resolution and interpersonal. Influencing others is about communicating with others. Almost every communication you observe could be better. Consider the three skills discussed below, how proficiently do you manage noise, ask for what you want, and confront? Is there room for improvement?

MANAGING NOISE

You can never control 100% of the potential distractions affecting your ability to communicate because of so many variables, some of which are found in the receiver's head! However, you can greatly increase your odds by quickly asking yourself, "What will interfere with my ability to influence?" Below is a checklist of situations qualifying as "noise" or distractions to the sending and receiving of messages:

Psychological: what's going on in the mind of the receiver; attention spans; receiver's impression of your skills

Physical: visual items (or people) that block receiver's vision or attention (i.e. your fly is down, someone famous walked in the room, etc.)

Hunger or pain: receiver's concentration is on his/her stomach not you

Stress: receiver is incapable of focusing on your message; receiver is too anxious, etc.

Environmental: visual distractions; inability to hear; temperature; time of day

One of the best ways to control such noise is to "SOFTEN it up." SOFTEN stands for Smiling, Open posture (no crossing of arms), Forward lean, Touch (or expression of warmth), Eye-contact, and Nod (remember gender concerns!). Practicing the proper non-verbal body postures called SOFTEN will help you to be more open, caring, and attractive. For example, holding private conversations in a private setting will decrease many of the distractions mentioned above. When you sit, invite someone else to sit. If you stand, avoid leaning on another object or wall.

ASKING FOR WHAT YOU WANT OR OTHERS NEED (ASSERTIVENESS)

We have talked about the confidence and high self-esteem associated with influence. *Zing!* individuals aren't afraid to be straightforward. *Assertiveness* is a style of communication designed to protect your basic human rights without violating another's basic human rights. It involves saying what you want without apology, clarifying your intentions, and being direct in your communications, whether you are standing up for yourself, asking for what you want, or acting for a greater cause.

All people have basic human rights to dignity, fair play, and freedom from judgment, oppression, and sarcasm. These rights are violated when they are treated with the following: inconsideration, insincerity, unethical behavior, manipulation, persuasion, betrayal, and force. To cross the line is to go from being assertive to aggressive, passive aggressive, or sarcastic styles of communication.

CONFRONTING OTHERS

Confrontation is the ability to bring something to someone else's attention to positively affect change. It is not bad or wrong to confront someone; rather, it is a valuable (and necessary) tool. You may be uncomfortable sharing important information like inadequate job performance, concern over a particular behavior, or the need for a colleague to "step up to the plate." But to not say something and let inappropriate behavior continue is an individual detractor. More importantly, you allow people who are ignorant, unethical, and harming others to continue such behavior. *Zing!* often means it's time to stand up for something. Confront because you care. I always ask the questions: What's the worst thing that's going to happen if I say something? Will this make the situation better or worse?

SKILL BUILDING LESSON

1. Go to Appendix A and complete the self-assessment titled "The Art of Communicating."
2. Practice improving your communication skills with strangers.
3. Manage your emotions during conversations.
4. Seek higher levels of reasoning as opposed to a higher volume. Avoid shouting.
5. Let silence happen.
6. Use phrases like "Let me be clear…" to signal your request.
7. Rearrange a room (or your office) so people find you approachable.
8. When confronting someone, don't sit behind an object (such as your desk)—this projects a power play.
9. Practice smiling at strangers.
10. Speak up for those who don't speak up for themselves.

"The exterior appearance can hide the interior truth."

19

Insight Fifteen:
The Attraction of Listening

*"About communication: I know you believe you understand
what you think I said. But, I'm not sure you realize that what you
heard is not what I meant."*
—Andy Warhol

The hardest aspect of listening is that you have to stop talking. That's right. You must close your mouth. You must stand—or sit—without saying a word. Sounds rather simple, doesn't it? It would be, if, during the process of listening, you not only heard what is being said, but what isn't being said! Effective listening is essential to maximizing your influence because it allows your friends, significant others, family members, co-workers, employees and strangers, to connect with you at an interpersonal level. When you actively listen, you make a large non-verbal statement about how important other people are to you.

People are very perceptive. To actually listen to the response to "How are you today?" speaks volumes. At a staff meeting, to follow a question with silence in order to listen for an answer also speaks volumes. To not complete others' sentences, cut people off, or look over someone's shoulder when they are speaking to you represent the greatest compliments (or signs of respect or praise) you can give another human being.

Say What?

In scientific communication models, the person whom you are speaking to is referred to as the "receiver." You are the "sender."

The primary goal of effective communication is enhanced comprehension. To understand others, you need to hear what they are directly (and indirectly) sending to you. I once heard listening defined as "an opportunity to think of what to say next." Yikes. In reality, listening is the ability to receive (i.e. understand) the meaning, content and emotion as it was intended by the sender(s).

Active listening is a learnable skill. Despite the fact you've been doing it all your life, you can still improve. To listen with accuracy requires the ability to be open, free from judgment, outwardly receptive, and actively engaged or attentive to others' thoughts as they communicate them. You need to hear what they are saying, not what you want to hear.

THE FABULOUS FIVE—PLUS ONE

If you want *Zing!* (and you do), you need to understand the complexity of listening comprehension. Once you get to know someone rather well, you can more easily work with their style of interpersonal communication. You will quickly assess their honesty. When you don't know what someone is trying to say, you must rely on other dependable indicators of meaning. I have identified six significant "targets" of listening. When you actively identify these six targets in every conversation you have, you greatly increase the odds you will eventually hit your mark!

BODY LANGUAGE

Abraham Lincoln once said: "What you do speaks so loud, I cannot hear what you say." He was aware of the enormous power of non-verbal communication. Words can be manipulated much easier than body language. Research on communication varies in the actual percentage assigned to the significance of body language, from 60% to over 90%. (My years of teaching communication skills make me favor a figure closer to 80%.) In any event, you listen more to someone's actions, positions, and eye-contact than you do to their words. When in a conversation, pay attention to the possible messages being sent through body language as suggested in the chart below.

MESSAGES OF MEANING

Crossed arms = desire to "protect" yourself, blocking your presence, emotional distance

Hands on hips = pride, honor, sense of security, desire to appear firm or unyielding

Standing on one foot = insecurity, insincerity of message, uncertainty, fear, intimidation

Crossing legs while standing = same as standing on one foot, uncomfortable

Pointing = sense of superiority, aggressiveness, "fight-or-flight" attitude

Touching someone's arm = desire to get closer, warmth, interest in deeper relationship, fondness

Hands in hair = flirtatious, desire to be more casual or intimate

Shoulders raised = defensive, stiff or rigid, uncomfortable, unsure of self

Leaning against something = unsure of position, casual attitude

Walking slowly = weighed down, burdened, unhappy, hopeless

Walking quickly = free, nervous, happy, determined, angry

Smiling = comfortable, interested in establishing a relationship

Tight face = angry, tense, stressed, distant

Eye-contact = honesty, emotion, avoidance, or engagement

CONTENT

The second target to look for in effective listening is the actual content of the communication or words being spoken. For example, is the sender making an effort to impress you with his/her vocabulary? Is he/she refraining from using profanity? Both actions communicate a desire to look favorable. Conversely, be aware when a receiver responds with the use of slang or inside jokes. This may be a sign that they are not letting you into their club! In reality, they are putting you in your place.

EMOTION

No matter how skilled you are at interpersonal communication, emotion is often difficult to read. You have to respond to the emotion of a comment before you respond to the content. When both emotion and content are congruent, you are most likely getting accurate information. However, if you observe "nervous energy" when someone is talking to you, don't ignore it. Ask yourself, "Why is this person nervous? Should I trust the information? What can I do to address the source of his/her anxiety?" As previously noted, *Zing!* requires honesty. The honesty of your communication lives in the emotion of a statement rather than in the words.

TONE

Tone is the *inflection* communicated in the message. Tone involves rate of response, the sound (or pitch) of the voice, and/or emphasis on certain words. For example, a fast rate can indicate panic, anxiety, or excitement. A slow rate can indicate sadness, shock, or confusion. A high-pitched voice usually coincides with the emotions of a fast rate of speech and a low-pitched voice with slow rate of speech. Emphasis on certain words can indicate sarcasm, anger, or even humor. Undoubtedly, tone is tricky to "hear," so you must take into account as many targets as you can grasp at one time.

GENDER AND CULTURAL DIFFERENCES

The role of gender and cultural differences as targets for effective listening deserve an entire chapter. Don't underestimate their significance! Research conducted by communication expert and author Dr. Deborah Tannen in *The Argument Culture* concludes there are gender differences in ways of speaking between men and women. For example, studies prove men believe women nod to show agreement, whereas women nod to show they are listening! Can you see how this understanding fosters more accurate communication? To learn more examples, I encourage you to read about gender issues in communication.

Similarly, understanding cultural differences in communication styles can greatly affect your ability to hear what is truly being said. For example, the Hispanic culture is dynamic, vivacious and expressive. Loud does not mean rude. Talking over one another also is not considered rude. Yelling or arguing isn't interpreted as violent or uncivil. Once the argument has ended, no grudges are held. It's over. In other cultures, this would not be the case.

EYE-CONTACT

The final target of eye-contact speaks volumes. When you look into someone's eyes, you can see sadness, joy, commitment, intensity, wisdom, humor, loneliness, happiness, longing, desire and/or so much more. To be an effective listener requires looking directly from your eyes to someone else's. This is often threatening because truth is found in the eyes. I'm fascinated by recent research on the predictive value of rate of blinking and dishonesty in message. Specifically, blinking rate increases when someone is being dishonest.

Another predictive tool indicating the validity of someone's words was shared by a former colleague who handled judicial affairs at a university. She said, "If you want to know if someone just told you the truth, discuss the issue at hand: if they are skilled liars, they will maintain eye-contact with you. Then, change the topic. If they immediately look away from you, they were lying." She further explained that in her experience, individuals can concentrate on maintaining eye-contact as long as they need to support their deceit. When they think they no longer need to keep up the front, their sub-conscious reacts by forcing their eyes to look away out of shame.

SKILL BUILDING LESSON

1. Go to Appendix A and complete the self-assessment titled "What Did You Hear?"
2. The most effective means of increasing your listening comprehension in interpersonal communications is to use paraphrasing. The art of paraphrasing is the art of playing back what you just heard someone to say to you in your own words. You can respond to someone's comment (and above mentioned targets) with the prefix: "I hear you saying…" followed by a brief summary. Or you can say: "Sounds to me as if…" followed by your take of their remarks. A conversation is like a ping-pong match. You want to continually give back what you were just given.
3. Control for potential distractions (i.e. environmental and psychological noise).

4. Interpret messages being spoken through the content, body language, and tone of speaker.
5. Hold important conversations when you are most attentive.
6. Learn about the cultural and gender differences in communication.
7. If communicating with women, nod during your conversation to validate that you are listening.
8. If communicating with men, say: "I understand" during your conversation to validate that you are listening.
9. Sit in the front row of class or closest to the person speaking.
10. If someone speaks in a manner you can't understand, politely ask him/her to slow down and/or speak up with more clarity.
11. When speaking to someone significantly taller or shorter, be seated.
12. Use the word but cautiously—it usually negates anything spoken before it.
13. Lean forward or inward when you want a conversation to continue.
14. When you are too personally distracted to listen effectively, honor the other person by saying: "I'm very interested in hearing your comments; however, I cannot give you my full attention right now. Can we reschedule?" This is far better than appearing uninterested.

"You can't move people to action unless you first move them with emotion. The heart comes before the head."
—John C. Maxwell

Insight Sixteen:
The Pull of the Podium

"Before I start speaking, I have something important to say."
—Yogi Berra

Imagine the pomp and circumstance of one of the most memorable commencement exercises in history. The scene is Oxford University. Under a nearby tent, a brass quartet plays Voltaire. To your right, someone fusses with his camera. Behind you, a little girl plays with her long braid as her grandmother leans over and whispers, "Settle down." Something great is about to happen. The graduates enter in a formal march. However, all eyes are fixed on the party leading the processional. After a series of traditional remarks, the audience leans forward in anticipation for the commencement speaker. Even the graduates appear focused on something other than their own success. On cue, Winston Churchill stands and walks with purpose to the podium. He says, "Never, never, never give up." Then, he sits back down. It is one of the most famous speeches ever delivered.

What do Ronald Reagan, Elizabeth Dole, John F. Kennedy, Jr., Gloria Steinem, Reverend Billy Graham, and Susan B. Anthony have in common? All were known for their exceptional oratory skills. Their success and achievements were due in large part to their ability to persuade their audiences to act.

Learning to Speak

One of my life's greatest blessings is my friendship with Dr. Will Keim. He is a man of considerable *Zing!*. Dr. Keim is a father, husband, minister, author, educator, speaker and my former mentor. In my opinion, he is one (if not *the*) best speaker and educator in higher education today. Whenever he speaks, you are inspired to act or change the way you think. He clearly is pursuing his vision of inspiring young adults via the podium to build characters of service and leadership. Towards this goal, he recently co-founded with Curtis Zimmerman The Character Institute.[1] According to Dr. Keim, "The art of public speaking demands precision in detail, persuasion in appeal and passion in delivery." To have all three is truly a gift. However, effective public speaking is a learnable skill.

OBSERVE AND LISTEN TO GREAT SPEAKERS

By observing great speakers, you improve your ability to identify the consistent traits that make them great. While driving, I enjoy listening to audiotapes of great speakers. This practice teaches me to listen far beyond the content or words and attend to the manner of delivery, style, use of silence, and passion in their voices. Dr. Martin Luther King, Jr. not only mastered all of these components, but possessed an incredible ability to use rhetoric to literally change the world. Word combinations like "valley of despair" or "divine dissatisfaction" create a picture in your mind and inspire emotion in your soul.

REHEARSE

The more you speak, the more you improve your speaking skills. Have you ever listened to someone speak and became nervous for them? Practice is the one thing that will improve your speaking ability. You can read all the books you want, hire a coach, but the only true way to get better at speaking in front of others is to actually speak in front of others!

SPEAK FROM YOUR HEART

Practice is what has helped our current president do better (yet not great) at the podium. He does his best, however, when he speaks less from a teleprompter and more from his heart. To this day, George W. Bush continues to struggle with a non-flowing speech pattern and sloppy pronunciation. You can clearly tell when he has practiced a speech and when he addresses an audience without the practice he requires. To his credit, however, he is not making up as many new words as he used to (i.e. "mis-underestimate") and is avoiding words he struggles with, such as "nuclear" (he says "nu-cu-lar"). I chuckled after the 2003 State of the Union address when commentators, almost in a sigh of relief, said: "President Bush came off as presidential this evening." (Was there another option?)

It's not easy to speak when the stakes are so high. In fact, I make up words all the time while speaking publicly, but I'm not President of the United States. When you are the president, the CEO of a company, the "face" of an organization, or running for political office, there is an expectation of podium performance. (It comes with the job.) Your ability to *Zing!* at the podium is a requirement for your life and leadership.

THE BENEFITS OF PUTTING YOURSELF OUT THERE

The true pull of the podium is that it gives you an opportunity to honor those you are blessed to serve by informing them, recognizing their talents, inspiring them to greater achievements, bringing them to a shared mission, and asking them to consider different points of view. Thousands of professional speakers, politicians, and celebrities live in America today. But where are the visionary voices? The answer is closer to you than you think. Survey after survey I conduct with my audiences reveal that they are turning to people in their more immediate environments, schools, organizations, jobs, communities, and local governments for lessons on life and leadership. They are listening to and seeking visionary thinkers, articulate philanthropists and people willing to take a stand. You can be the difference. Speak up!

Your ability to pull your audience's attention will benefit your ZQ in many ways. Consider the following:

You will become extremely perceptive of your audience's non-verbal communication. For example, if you fail to read your audience, you might continue to talk after your allocated time has run out. You might miss people looking at their watches, fixing their coats, rocking in their seats and looking annoyed that their time hasn't been respected. My first lesson on public speaking is "never, never, never speak longer than assigned!"

You will learn instinctively what methods, rhetoric, and style are most effective at evoking emotion in others. All oratory is persuasive. If you can't inspire your audience to listen and act, you are just a talking head.

You have an opportunity to think about and organize your thoughts prior to speaking. The organization of a speech is a learnable skill. An important lesson to learn when writing a speech is to be concise, direct, captivating, and entertaining, while making no more than five major points.

You get to experiment with a more entertaining or passionate you. Many speaking programs will teach you to stay at the podium. As I noted earlier, I'm five feet tall—or short. I am not comfortable when talking from a structure that is taller than I am! It is an individual detractor. By using humor and experimenting with various mediums and use of stage space, you develop your personal style.

You build a positive reputation by doing something most people are afraid to try. According to many sources, public speaking is the number one fear (number two being death) of people. Have the courage to give your ideas a forum of expression and the light shines directly on your life and leadership for all to see. This is a good thing.

You become more confident in your abilities. Improvement comes with effort—even if it doesn't go well the first few times. Learn from what works and what needs work.

You keep your job or get a job. Public speaking plays a more significant role in our life's job description than most are willing to accept. Don't let your fear or past performances stop you from stepping up to the plate, running for town office, or moving up the corporate ladder. Effective speaking requires risk-taking.

CHARACTERISTICS OF EFFECTIVE SPEAKERS

Whenever I have the chance, I listen to other speakers. I make notes on what I like about their programs and styles and what doesn't work for me. Characteristics consistently associated with effective speakers include the following:

- Well-prepared
- Humorous
- Stick to the allocated time frame
- Present original thoughts
- Don't make excuses for being "bad"
- Voices change in volume, tone and rate
- Tell personal stories
- Comfortable with silence
- Play on different emotions
- Refrain from condescending attitude
- Appearances are appropriate for setting
- Enjoy being on stage
- Refrain from criticizing their audience or offending even one person
- Respectful
- Avoid holding a glass of water and/or shaking it
- Thank sponsors or show appreciation to their audience
- Don't read a speech
- Maintain eye-contact with the audience
- Interact with audience members prior to the program
- Smile

CHARACTERISTICS OF EFFECTIVE SPEECHES

An exceptional presentation can sometimes save a poorly-written speech. Audience members are so entertained they overlook a lack of substance in favor of being amused. Why not have both; great delivery and a great speech? The more consistently you incorporate the following characteristics of effective speeches, the higher your ZQ:

- Hook the audience in the first few seconds
- Cover five or less main points
- Back up points with relevant stories, examples, or statistics
- Sequence points so they flow logically
- Inspire a variety of emotions
- Explain the "contextual relevancy" of the topic to audience
- Close with a connected hook used to open the speech
- Include follow-up by referring a web-site
- Leave the audience wanting more
- Provide accurate references to quoted material
- Reiterate the five or less major points
- Topic is appropriate to the setting
- Use a variety of mediums (between two to five) to make a point

SKILL BUILDING LESSON

1. Go to Appendix A and complete the self-assessment titled "Public Speaking Homework."
2. Know your audience. For example, I like to know things like male/female ratio, level of education, expectations, general professional experience, and motivation for attending the program. Adjust your program to meet the needs of the environment and audience.
3. Give people a chance to warm up to you; progress from non-threatening material to more challenging topics.
4. Keep your language and thoughts one step (not ten) above your audience. Don't make people feel stupid in your attempt to sound smart.
5. Draw from the audience's experiences whenever possible.
6. Write your comments in outline form and staple the outline together. Practice from your outline until it fits on a napkin.
7. Prepare your speeches and presentations for the possibility that technology will be unreliable.

8. When using PowerPoint, never look directly at the presentation screen. Get a remote and use your laptop as your personal screen with the presentation screen behind you.
9. Never criticize a response or answer from an audience member. However, keep the standard of responses at a high level by challenging inappropriate remarks.
10. Compliment your audience whenever possible.
11. Avoid profanity at all costs. Respect your audience.
12. To make your points, consider a host of different mediums including magic tricks, music, group work, poems, demonstrations, a reading from Chicken Soup for the Soul, brief video clip, or questions to the audience.
13. Remember: No one knows what your outline contained but you!

*"One can never consent to creep
when one feels an impulse to soar."*
—Helen Keller

21

INSIGHT SEVENTEEN:
THE BUILDING OF RELATIONSHIPS

"The more people you know and who know you in a positive way, the more likely it is that you will know the right person at the right time for the right reason to take advantage of the right opportunity."
—*Brian Tracy*

As a child, I identified with Casper the Friendly Ghost. I thought it would be rather exciting to float through walls, listen in on conversations and fly above houses. I could go wherever I wanted, whenever I wanted. Being invisible seemed appealing. But by the time I hit the sixth grade, it didn't seem like so much fun anymore. In fact, to be unnoticed was devastating. When did you first realize that you wanted to be noticed?

Individuals with *Zing!* notice everyone: tall, short, fat, thin, young, and old. To increase your *influence*, you need to make people feel like they matter. You can say "Hello" and still make someone feel invisible. Charismatic exchanges go beyond dismissive greetings to more genuine interactions. Your goal is to always leave people feeling like human beings and more worthy in your presence, regardless of their position—or your position.

Early in my professional career, I didn't get it. One of the greatest individual detractors in my charismatic portfolio was the manner in which I treated my secretary. Although she worked every day to ensure that my work was done, I never really noticed her or made her feel as important as I could. Sometimes I would say, "Good morning!" and, in the same breath, ask, "Would you do this for me, please?" I focused on my needs, instead of her needs. No *Zing!* whatsoever. My ignorance of Dale Carnegie's lessons on "how to win friends and influence others" also included the non-charismatic practice of calling someone to obtain information and neglecting to ask about their life or make them feel valued before I politely asked for what I needed. I forgot what it felt like to be Casper—to be invisible.

QUESTIONS OF LEADERSHIP

Do you make people feel invisible by accident or design? Do you notice, acknowledge, and treat the person who crosses your children at the crosswalk every day the same way you notice, acknowledge, and treat the school's principal? Does the person who empties your trash can at the office get the same respect and acknowledgement as the person who sits across from you at your staff meeting? Simply knowing someone's name is not the same as knowing them. My mother used to say, "To have a good friend, you must be a good friend." Your ability to walk into a room of 100 people and make each one feel like they are the most important person is indicative of the value you place on building relationships.

THE REAL TRAITS OF REAL RELATIONSHIPS

If you didn't have to, would you hang out with you? Would you want to be supervised by you? Would you want to share an office with you? Would you want to serve on a committee with you? Would you marry you? Knowing yourself is an important step in establishing meaningful relationships. Hopefully, Groucho Marx was kidding when he said: "I would never join a club that would have me as a member."

THE DESIRE TO UNDERSTAND OTHERS

In his bestselling book *The Seven Habits of Highly Successful People*, Steven Covey does a wonderful job of discussing the complexities of life and leadership as seven distinct behaviors or "habits." They include: Be proactive; Begin with the end in mind; Put first things first; Think win/win; Seek first to understand, then be understood; Synergize; and Sharpen the saw. Covey notes, "The key to valuing [the mental, emotional, and psychological difference between people] is to realize that all people see the world, not as it is, but as

142

they are." People who *Zing!* hold a higher standard for relationships and interactions with others because they understand this concept. Thus, if you want to increase the quality of your relationships, increase the quality you bring to your relationships! Work harder at understanding and appreciating the differences or individuality of people. Go beyond tolerance to make others feel worthy. After all, you "tolerate" a headache until the aspirin kicks in! Consider the following factors that determine others' willingness to associate with you.

OPEN-MINDEDNESS

Are you open to your co-workers' ideas, thoughts, and emotions, or do you shut them off and out? I recall having someone say to me once, "I don't want to talk about that; let's talk about what I want to talk about." Thinking he was joking, I laughed. Unfortunately, as I later learned, this high ranking self-proclaimed charismatic leader apparently said this in many of his conversations. His unwillingness to be open to other topics was a significant individual detractor. Be open to not only a diverse topic of conversation, but all of the other differences people can bring to a relationship like travel experiences, cultural upbringing, family, gender interests, educational pursuits and so on.

TRUSTWORTHY

Do you gossip? If you speak negatively of others, you tell the person with whom you are currently speaking that you can't be trusted to not speak negatively of him/her. Relationships require what I call the "comfort of connection." In the Conger, Kanungo and Menon study of follower effects (1998), "trust in a leader" was one of the variables linked to charismatic leadership.[1] In their discussion, they concluded: "The charismatic leader also builds follower trust through a demonstrated concern for follower needs, personal sacrifices, and unconventional expertise. . . They transform their concern for followers' needs into a total dedication and commitment to a common cause they share, and they express these qualities in a disinterested and selfless manner."

LACK SELF-IMPORTANCE OR EGO

I've mentioned earlier the role of ego as an individual detractor.

To build relationships, check your ego at the door. Replace it with humility. Let your talents speak for themselves. Remember: if you have to tell someone just how good you are, you're not all that good!

FULL ENGAGEMENT

When in the presence of others, it matters whether you are happy to be there. You can demonstrate this by adding to the conversation, acknowledging their presence, and non-verbal language. Have you ever watched some men shop with their wives? These are not happy guys. I speak from experience. If you don't want to be somewhere, don't go! Despite your good intentions, you'll be a downer. Your lack of active engagement, smiling, participation, and slouching posture will pick up where your silence and grunts leave off.

OPEN THE DOOR FOR FUTURE CONTACTS

Oftentimes, the one determining factor between ongoing relationships and one-time encounters is your ability to follow up. Instead of saying, "We should get together," or "I hope to see you again," consider saying, "I've enjoyed meeting you; would you like to get together for coffee this week?" Always have a business card ready to give away. Even if you don't have an official title, you can have a business card that contains your contact information (specifically, your name, address, phone number, and email address). Keeping your cards in the box on your shelf isn't going to help a potential new contact remember you. Make a good impression from the start. I recommend using a leather business card case that allows you to keep your cards on one side and "incoming" cards on the other. This also protects your cards so they don't look like you've had them in your wallet for three years!

INVITE ONE, INVITE ALL

Remember that charisma is about reverence and positive influence. When with a group, don't invite one person for lunch and exclude all the other potential Caspers standing there. Don't say you hope to see someone again if you really hope you'll never see them again!

FOLLOW UP WITH CARE AND CONSIDERATION

Another way to look at follow-up is to view it as nurturing your relationships. How can you make your relationships grow and how do you sustain them? For example, if you want to meet someone for coffee, don't ask the other person(s) to call you—you make the first move and honor them with a phone call!

Elizabeth George, author of *Life Management for Busy Women* comments, "it takes time, care, love, and money to nurture our relationships." She recommends, "purchasing little cards, small gifts, something that shouts out that person's name when we walk by, something [the other person] collects, uses, loves, enjoys, reads, and appreciates." Likewise, sending thank-you cards goes along way to express your desire to show someone your appreciation.

THE COMPANY YOU KEEP

"You are known by the company you keep." Your associates reflect your values, vision, and self-esteem. If you want to know where you'll be in five years, check out who you are hanging around with now. Be willing to let go of dysfunctional relationships or spend less time with people who "suck the energy right out of you." I give you permission to throw out someone's business card if you want to. You deserve to be happy. They deserve to be happy.

THE DENNEY STAGES OF BUILDING RELATIONSHIPS

Understanding the process of establishing relationships will help you to connect and establish more meaningful relationships. You will also increase the probability of more authentic exchanges—whichever stage you are in. As suggested by the chart below, the important thing is to be true to yourself as well as to the people you meet. If someone in your presence starts to go down a path that is morally inappropriate, you don't have to agree, laugh, or stay in that exchange. Don't lower your standards to gain a "friend" or win favor with someone. Instead, invite that person to raise his/her standards.

Stage of Relationship Building	Risk Level	Commitment Level	Nature of Conversations
1. Pseudo-Exchange (How can I make this person comfortable in my presence?)	None	Conditional	Superficial, introductions
2. Exploration (What do I need to know to determine if we can have a relationship?)	Low	Unsure	Approach more complex topics, remove barriers of communication, learning
3. Real Deal Decision (Is this a relationship I will take to a higher level?)	High	Move up or down	Important topics, look at values, vision of the future
4. Synergy (Am I a better person for knowing this person?)	Low	Something has clicked and you mutually benefit from the relationship	Most topics are acceptable, deeper level of conversation, real communication, varied emotions displayed
5. Trust (How can we become better people together?)	None	Unconditional	Sense of safety, motives pure and understood, failures are forgiven

GIVE IT TIME

Trust is the most developed stage of a relationship. When you aren't honest in your communications, or misread the commitment in a relationship, you interfere with another person's sense of comfort and his/her ability to be authentic. Because the process of relationship building is outward (not inward) and moves from what's on the surface (or small talk) to the inner realm of trust, give your first encounters time to turn into relationships—*if* you want them to.

SHARE APPROPRIATE INFORMATION

Another use of the above chart is to suggest the benefits of holding back how much you disclose too soon in a relationship. Err on the side of being too formal. Unless invited to use someone's first name, use their proper name (i.e. Dr. Hunter).

THE DIFFICULTIES OR COMPLEXITIES OF RELATIONSHIPS

The reasons why someone might resist your overtures towards a relationship are complicated. Co-workers, for instance, have to work within an organizational structure and changing office dynamics. Supervisory roles represent potential struggles with authority, competition, and evaluation. When anyone has authority (real or perceived) over someone else, the playing field is not equal. When you are in a position of authority over someone else, you need to recognize the potential limits on your relationship and allow it to benefit the greater good. Deeper relationships are built when both parties are free to give and receive in the relationship.

In addition, you might not get to choose what your relationship becomes or if you will interact again. Other factors, such as the setting, circumstance, or hidden agendas might mask the making of a true relationship. For example, during a recent conversation with a new friend, she confessed to resisting my initial overtures of friendship. Further conversation revealed that all of our meetings had been at social events where I tend to be very outgoing and she prefers to talk with people she knows well. To *Zing!* in your relationships may require meeting someone on "neutral" (not beige) ground.

ACTIVITIES OF RELATIONSHIP BUILDING

NETWORK EFFECTIVELY

Networking is the establishing of mutually beneficial relationships. Networking expert and author of *The Networking Survival Guide*, Diane Darling notes: "Networking is building relationships before you need them." The key to *Zing!* networking is to let others know how you can help them. In addition, you must continually create ways of maintaining communication with someone after you meet them. Whether this is a monthly cup of coffee, occasional phone call or card, if you want someone to remember you, you need to first remember them.

HAVE A FIRM HANDSHAKE

There they are... at the end of your arms. Conveniently located and frequently ignored. One of the best ways to welcome or invite someone into your life is to extend your hand until it meets firmly with the other person's hand. If you have small hands, you need to squeeze a little tighter. If you have big hands, soften up on your grip. Maintain contact for a minimum of five seconds.

To make your greetings warmer, consider holding your handshake even longer and placing your other hand over it.

IDENTIFY YOUR INNER CIRCLE

Many high achieving individuals maintain an "inner circle" or small group of equally successful people to serve as spiritual guides, mentors, counselors, advisors and supporters. In many cases, their circle represents individuals who represent where they want to go (not where they've been). To think like a billionaire, for example, don't hang around with millionaires. Your inner circle should represent a diversity of support areas. Individuals to enrich the following areas of your life are suggested: financial, spiritual, emotional, grounding (or purpose), achievement (or career), and inspirational.

REMEMBER SOMEONE'S NAME

Ever forget someone's name as it is being introduced to you? Your name is like a key: offer it to others and invite them into your life and leadership. You want them to use it. Likewise, when someone offers you his/her name, use it! Below are a few sure bet tips on how to remember someone's name:

1. Repeat the name immediately upon hearing it so you learn to pronounce it correctly.
2. Focus on the first name only.
3. Don't go any further in your conversation until you can repeat the other person's name.
4. Use the name again in the first fifteen words of your conversation.
5. Ask for a business card to reinforce the spelling of their name.
6. Repeat their name during the conversation at least three times.
7. At the conclusion of your encounter, repeat their name

again, so it's the last thing you say.

8. Look down at their business card, after they leave.

You can also make it easier for someone to remember your name by referring to yourself in the third person during your conversation. It sounds silly, but it is an effective way of putting your name out there again so the other person or party can remember it.

ENGAGE IN SMALL TALK

Remember! A conversation is a ping pong game. Keep serving up open ended questions (i.e. questions beginning with how, why, what, and so on) and dig deeper. You can start with "Tell me what brings you here..." or "How have you spent your time..." Small talk does not have to be meaningless. It's talk. Your goal, however, is not to do all the talking! Here are some additional tips:

1. Pay a compliment early in the conversation.
2. Smile often.
3. Start sentences with "conversation triggers" such as: "Tell me about..." or "It's a beautiful day, what brings you here?" or "It's a pleasure to meet you. What are you hoping to do while you are here?"
4. Avoid looking down when silence occurs—instead, look directly in the other person's eyes.
5. If the other person is rather shy, help them out by saying, "I don't personally like these kinds of social events. Sometimes they make me feel uncomfortable. What kinds of events make you feel more relaxed?"
6. Use the environment to your advantage. What do you see that you can reference as a common denominator? For example, "I'm impressed by our surroundings. How do you find the architecture?" or "What a beautiful room. I admit to entering a room and deciding exactly what wall I will be taking down! I'm a big fan of interior design and renovation. How about you?"
7. Of course, remember to shake the hand of your small talk partner upon the greeting and after your conversation.

PAYING IT FORWARD

Establishing relationships is like giving a gift. You can often tell from the wrapping that you're going to like what's inside. The effective relationship builder hands out gifts all day long knowing they might not get anything in return, yet hoping the gift they shared will be passed on to someone else.

SKILL BUILDING LESSON

1. Go to Appendix A and complete the self-assessment titled "Relationship Potential 101."
2. Remember! Every encounter is a chance to make someone's day.
3. Be willing to create more meaningful exchanges and relationships.
4. Verbally express how you value your relationships with others.
5. Send a card or perform an act of kindness to someone you like.
6. Leave every conversation with a word of praise for the other person.
7. Find creative ways to keep the communication door open.
8. Always carry business cards.
9. At the end of a conversation, ask for someone else's business card.
10. Stand when shaking someone's hand, maintain eye-contact and smile.
11. Treat everyone with an equal amount of respect. No one should be made to feel like Casper the Friendly Ghost.
12. Make the effort to remember people's names.
13. Associate with people who can help you achieve your dreams.
14. Embrace diversity in your relationships.
15. Remember people's birthdays and special occasions.

"People in your presence should be made better people because of your presence."

22

INSIGHT EIGHTEEN: THE PUNCH OF HUMOR

Question: Why aren't you running in the gubernatorial race?
Comedian Steve Allen's response: Because I don't want to be a
gubernor.

Laugh and the whole world laughs with you. I don't know who made that statement but he/she understood the *Zing!* appeal of humor. Levity plays a wonderful role in drawing people together. I believe it's a universal language that transcends age, art, and cultural differences to bring joy and happiness to the world. If you don't believe that you are funny, you must at least believe you have the potential to bring joy and laughter to the world.

BENEFITS OF HUMOR

Humor does more than make people laugh. One of the greatest gifts you can give another human being is to bring them joy. You show others you care about them when you make them laugh. You make them feel worthy by creating playfulness, cheer, and happiness. Your light heartedness will be rewarded by their reactions. In fact, they might even return the favor!

THE LIFT OF LAUGHTER

Misery loves company and visa versa. Hopeful people will seek out those who lift them up, not bring them down. Funny people like to associate with people who make them laugh. Anyone who seeks enjoyment from life will quickly welcome a break from the stressors of life. Humor draws people to you socially and professionally.

ON A ROLL

Have you ever started to laugh and can't stop? What begins as a chuckle turns into roll-on-the- floor laughter. Your stomach tightens, your eyes tear and you make snorting noises with your nose. As you start to collect yourself, you grip your belly and take deep breaths. Your laughing fit leaves you much more susceptible to laughing again. I have often watched very effective speakers get their audience laughing and keep them laughing. A magical exchange takes place in which the audience members transform from a "show me what you've got" mentality to a "Wow! Keep making me laugh!" mentality. The best speeches I've ever given were ones in which I got on a roll and the audience's laughter inspired me to create even more humor – one fueled the other. *Zing!* comes alive with laughter.

PERSONAL GIFTS

Consider these additional benefits of bringing humor to the world around you:

You reveal your own humility when you laugh at yourself. The ability to laugh at your own stupidity and silliness brings people towards you because they see you as human and wonderfully flawed.

Levity can break tension, reduce stress and make people feel more relaxed. When appropriate, telling a joke or using humor to prevent tense exchanges or situations from escalating is masterful leadership. Laughter brings not only a psychological lift, but also a physiological lift. The chemicals released in your brain during laughter make you more relaxed, comfortable, and light-headed. When people are anxious, apprehensive, or nervous, use humor as a calming influence or distraction.

Humor reflects your intelligence and wit. The most successful stand up comics are extremely bright individuals. They have a sharp wit and a keen perceptiveness to their surroundings. When you tell sophomoric jokes, you will be viewed as immature. When you use a more sophisticated wit, you will demonstrate intelligence and maturity.

Humor keeps you from going insane. Humor protects you. Many of the funny individuals in our lives have learned to be funny as a defense mechanism against the world. Instead of retreating into themselves to escape the pain of a difficult childhood, for example, they projected their energies outward. When you use humor to move your life forward, you give yourself a gift.

Humor heals. Laughter is the best medicine. People who laugh live longer.

Using humor makes you a more effective conversationalist. People will want to engage in conversations with you when you appear comfortable enough to share your humor with them.

WHAT'S SO FUNNY?

It is theorized that laughter is like the brain "hiccupping." Your brain starts to follow a certain course of logic or reason or expectation and all of a sudden–hiccup–it registers something it didn't expect to get. Steve Allen discusses a similar explanation of laughter in his book *How to Be Funny: Discovering the Comic in You* when he notes how laughter is the result of: "the brain being forced to recognize an alternative explanation." You laugh because you expect one thing and get something else. Allen says, "…laughter is produced out of a sort of minor nervous explosion in the brain, a kind of short-circuit spark…the brain is momentarily startled… it's normal function interrupted. When you do the unexpected, you will make people laugh."

Humor relies on context and situation. Allen says,

"The funniest things are not jokes we hear on the radio or on movie screens, but the real-life social faux pas, slips of the tongue, fumblings and bumblings that amused human beings for millions of years before anyone ever thought of being funny on a professional basis… Nothing is inherently amusing of itself; humor lies only in particular contextual relationships."[1]

He cites an example of when he played the straight-man to an unpredictable studio audience.

This was a technique he mastered – live audience interaction. On one occasion, he asked a man, "What's your name?" In a reportedly calm voice, the man replied, "Boston, Massachusetts." At that very moment, he couldn't have said anything as funny as the audience member had just said in that situation. Allen notes the man's answer had "all the elements of true humor; it's ridiculous, absurd, entirely unpredictable, and comes as a lightning-quick surprise."

How to Trigger Laughter in Others

Humor is a direct line to positively influencing others. You can become a funnier human being if you are willing to experiment with new behaviors. As a speaker, I've studied numerous methods of facilitating laughter. Along the way I've discovered the following things make people laugh:

- Hearing contagious laughter
- Making fun of yourself
- Telling jokes that are appropriate, harmless, and clean.
- "Ad-libbing" with strangers
- Witty word choice
- Using satire to express different points of view, like the political satire of Jon Stewart
- Visual humor like a sketch or prop
- Engaging in or watching silliness or "child's play."
- Simple actions like the antics of Ellen DeGeneres or Lucille Ball

Finding the Humor in a Room That Leaked

I recently found myself speaking at a "mandatory motivational" meeting of over six hundred students at a university in Missouri. It was pouring rain, end of the year exams were scheduled that same week, and students had to sign in to receive credit for attending my lecture. In other words, not a receptive audience.

Being the perceptive speaker that I am, I picked up on the many clues being left of the sentiment of my audience. First, upon entering, many students sat at a round table, faced their backs to the stage and took out their books. One group began sewing ribbons for their upcoming philanthropy. Another group actively sought out the tables furthest from the stage. Yet another group made non-discrete comments like, "This is going to suck."

I now had a choice. I could run and run fast. Or, I could play. Table by table, I stopped and made small talk with audience members trying intentionally to make them laugh. They did. At one table, I literally sat down and said, "Man, think it could rain a little more?" The gentlemen at the table said, "Hey, if it did those ceiling tiles over the stage would definitely crash down on the speaker. How cool!" I laughed and then turned towards the stage. Yes, the ceiling was leaking over the podium…

Instinctively, I turned back to my new best friends and said, "So, what's going on here tonight?" Leaning back in his chair and placing his feet on the table, one young man said, "Some speaker about car wrecks. We have to be here. It's mandatory." Further inquiry revealed that the last mandatory speaker came to fulfill a liability requirement for drunk driving prevention and showed a video with dead bodies. I got up, went to the stage, smiled at my companions and introduced myself. Clasping the hand-held microphone, I began to tell the story of my trip from the East Coast to the university, describing in detail the three planes, decreasing in size as I came closer to Missouri, and the declining age of the pilots, noting the last pilots were wearing braces and carrying lunch boxes.

My story continued with a lively description of the hour and a half drive to the hotel. I noted how disappointing it was in comparison to Boston driving, followed by a demonstration of Boston drivers: the changing of lanes, stopping in the center lane for no apparent reason, and cutting people off. My audience watched, attentive and amused. I even heard an occasional murmur of laughter.

Finally, after complaining about the rain, the tornado watch, and standing in my hotel room looking out at a potential natural disaster, I said, "It was at this point I really, really, really didn't want to come here tonight." And then, just as silence overtook the room, I quipped, "But, it was mandatory. I had to show up."

The leadership speech went fine.

We were all living that scenario at the same time. Rather than attempt to ignore the obvious, I used it to my advantage. The other option was to begin my remarks with, "I know you don't want to be here. But, I'm going to speak an hour of your lifetime away."

When you make a conscious decision to play instead of fight or to look for the humor in a potentially humorless or challenging situation, People will respond positively to your attempts to make them happy.

THE APPROPRIATENESS OF HUMOR

The tricky thing about humor is to avoid going overboard to the point of poor taste or no taste. Experimenting with humor can be risky, especially if your humor is inappropriate despite what *you* think. Your audience's opinion of appropriate humor matters; otherwise, what you think is funny suddenly becomes an individual detractor.

DENNEY'S RULES ON HUMOR

- Never, under any circumstance, use male or female bashing to make people laugh.
- Experiment with different jokes or personal stories.
- Delivery and content just as important as the content of a personal anecdote or joke.
- Physically "get into" your story or joke. If it involves someone walking, for instance, mimic walking as you paint the visual picture.
- Never make people laugh at the expense of someone other than yourself.
- If you are using an anecdote from another source, don't pass it off as yours. Properly reference someone else's creativity.
- Take the hint. If someone is kind enough to tell you "that wasn't funny," believe them.
- When in doubt, leave it out.
- Avoid crossing the line between "fabrication" and "exaggeration."
- Practice your jokes or monologues in front of other people before using them in high stakes situations.

A WORD ON SARCASM

Sarcasm is the attempt to be funny by being "subtly aggressive" at someone else's expense. It should only be used when directed at inanimate objects not people. When directed at a person or group, sarcasm is a form of aggression. It violates their basic human rights by tricking the other person, or group, into believing they aren't being picked on, attacked, or insulted. In reality, that's exactly what you are doing.

Skill Building Lesson

1. Go to Appendix A and complete the self-assessment titled "A Punch of Humor."
2. Believe you can learn to be funny.
3. Pick up a book about humor or whose content is humorous. Steve Allen, for example, has authored over forty-five books. Some are instructional; others are murder mysteries with creative and humorous twists.
4. Observe and imitate someone who is funny.
5. Go to a comedy club.
6. Watch the better satirists and comedians on television. Learn from them.
7. Hang around funny people.
8. Listen to comedy CDs or tapes.
9. Observe the playfulness and silliness of children.
10. Write your own jokes – or recreate your version of history.
11. Look for humor every day.
12. Ask people about their funniest moments. Make it a topic of conversation.

"Allowance is what you get for saying you cleaned your room."
—Kaitlin Elizabeth Denney

23

INSIGHT NINETEEN: THE APPEAL OF PLAYFULNESS

"The child is in me still…and sometimes not so still."
—*Fred Rogers*

It's a beautiful day in your neighborhood, won't you be my neighbor?

These words were the trademark of Mr. Fred Rogers. His red cardigan sweater symbolized a shift from the formal to the comfortable. It was his invitation to play. To not like Mr. Rogers wouldn't stop him from liking you. His living room became our living room. His purpose in life was to provide children with a source of entertainment founded in such values as love, compassion, education, and good spirited fun. To fulfill this purpose, Mr. Rogers was a creator, composer, puppeteer, and musician. He earned a graduate degree in child development and became an ordained Presbyterian minister. He also founded the non-profit organization Family Communications, Inc. to ensure his vision of children's television programming would endure.

Despite his numerous recognitions, including being inducted into the Television Hall of Fame, Mr. Roger's greatest legacy is the way he made children feel when they watched *Mister Rogers' Neighborhood* on PBS. This is where Mr. Rogers clearly loved to play. After his death in 2002, Mr. Rogers' wife compiled and published a wonderful collection of his favorite sayings and quotes. By reading *The World According to Mr. Rogers*, you begin to understand how he managed to positively influence generations of Americans. Mr. Rogers speaks to the seriousness of play when he said,

"Play does seem to open up another part of the mind that is always there, but that, since childhood, may have become closed off and hard to reach. When we treat children's play as seriously as it deserves, we are helping them feel the joy that's to be found in the creative spirit. We're helping ourselves stay in touch with that spirit, too. It's the things we play with and the people who help us play that make a great difference in our lives." [1]

THE SERIOUSNESS OF BEING PLAYFUL

Carrying this playfulness into your adulthood will significantly benefit your ability to influence. *Playfulness* – also known as a sense of adventurousness or creative spirit, is identified in numerous sources as an appealing and overridingly consistent trait found in successful individuals and leaders. In their most recently released book *Geeks and Geezers*, Warren Bennis and Robert Thomas define the concept of playfulness as neoteny.[2]

Bennis and Thomas discovered that every one of their "geezers" (leaders who were 25 years old between 1945–1954) had the: "wonderful qualities associated with youth; curiosity, playfulness, eagerness, fearlessness, warmth, energy." These traits kept them hungry for knowledge and discovery. They also note: "The capacity for uncontaminated wonder, ultimately, is what distinguishes the successful from the ordinary, the happily engaged players from whatever era from the chronically disappointed and malcontent."

FISH TALES

Another testament to the significance of play is the popularity of a simple approach to life called the "Fish Philosophy" which first appeared in *Fish* by authors Stephen C. Lundin, Ph.D., John Christensen, and Harry Paul.

SOUNDS FISHY

The Fish Philosophy was inspired by Dr. Lundins' youthful experiences as a camp counselor for children with Muscular Dystrophy, cancer, and other significant health conditions. It took almost forty years before he was able to write the many life lessons he had learned about courage, determination, suffering, joy, life, and death, while at camp. He iden-

tifies the catalyst as a local fish market.

While filming a documentary in Seattle, Dr. Lundin and his friend, a video photographer, went to a local fish market to buy fish. Customers flocked to this particular market in recognition of its cooperative, productive, and playful atmosphere. As he observed the silliness and spirit around him, Dr. Lundin was reminded of the same themes present during his earlier days at camp. The Fish Philosophy was born. The FISH approach to life recommends you do the following:

Play.
Make their day.
Be there.
Choose your attitude.

Dr. Lundin's early observation about human behavior stood the test of time: When you make something fun (even something as potentially disgusting or slimy as beheading fish) you will attract people to the activity, and this includes its purpose, planners and participants.

CHARACTERISTICS OF PLAYFULNESS

Playfulness is an attitude as well as an activity. When you make play part of your character, you make a decision to view the world from the eyes of a child. Consider the following characteristics of playful people:

- Laugh at their own silliness
- Create adventure
- Take the road less traveled
- Stop to smell the roses
- Fill their time with productive activities
- Make hobbies part of their every day
- Curious about how things work
- Ask "what if" questions
- Look for more than one answer
- Invite other people into their "sandbox"

- See colors as opposed to black and white (or beige)
- Kind hearted and warm
- Forgiving of failure – yours and theirs
- Intentionally and unintentionally make others laugh
- Are hungry for knowledge
- Pplay games
- Possess positive energy
- Enjoy recreation, activity, and movement

LEADERSHIP THROUGH PLAYFULNESS

One of the most charismatic and influential individuals I know is a vice-president of student affairs at a major university in New York State by the name of Dr. Dennis Black. He has a national reputation for his work in legal affairs in higher education. Despite the seriousness of his subject area, Dr. Black embraces playfulness as a leadership tool. He uses it masterfully to put others at ease and relieve potentially stressful situations. When combined with his ability to see the bigger picture, Dr. Black inspires the best in others.

A DISNEY DON'T

I first met Dr. Black while attending a conference in Orlando. It was hosted at one of the beautiful Disney properties and so I had decided to take my oldest child Jake with me. He was six years old. Before being able to take my son to Disney World, I had a speech to give. Little did I know, I was the one who was going to learn an important lesson about life and leadership: You can judge another's sense of playfulness by observing their interactions with children.

While I was in the middle of giving a speech, Jake was ready to go to the park. At the least, he wanted to leave the banquet facility and let his wishes be known to the entire audience. Confusion erupted as the conference director carried my screaming son out of the room. Within seconds, I went from being in control to feeling overwhelming concern for my son, combined with a big dose of embarrassment. I attempted to finish my speech.

Afterwards, as the room cleared, I looked for my child. A quick glance to my left did the trick. With big smiles on their faces, pant legs rolled up, and two ties around their heads (Ninja Turtle style) Jake and the afternoon keynote speaker, Dr. Black, skipped towards me. I developed instant admiration for Dr. Black's uncontaminated wonder and willingness to play with Jake.

In that same situation, would you "jump in with both feet" or would you be too busy talking about the awkwardness of the situation? Would you have been offering to help or starting a "Worst Mother of the Year" petition on my behalf? Dr. Black's playful response spoke volumes about his approach to leadership. Playfulness is an effective tool in overriding competing forces to positively influence others, and in some cases (like Mr. Rogers, Walt Disney, Charles Schultz, and Barney creator Sheryl Leach) turns into a lasting legacy.

BENEFITS OF PLAYFULNESS

When you bring play, adventure, and curiosity into your daily life, you will both give and receive many gifts. Specifically, being playful has the following positive outcomes:

- Spreads joy to those around you
- Creates an environment of creativity and productivity
- Demonstrates a consistent desire to turn negatives into positives
- Makes you approachable
- Allows people to risk failure (and success) without penalty
- Makes you more imaginative and innovative
- Creates a sense of intrigue and curiosity about you
- Encourages others to be more playful and curious
- Results in a higher quantity of ideas

MAKING THE PLAY AND CREATIVITY CONNECTION

To make a difference in this world, find a playful way to accomplish your goals. If the projector breaks down in the middle of your presentation, is your ability to *Zing!* out the window as well? If you arrive at an organizational meeting to find twice as many people as expected with half as many chairs, are you stumped? Solve the problems in your life from the perspective of youthful vision or play. Look through the eyes of a child–play, create, and do the unexpected.

HOW TO PLAY

When you are playful, you can always answer the question: "So, what do you want to do?" Boredom is neither an option nor part of your repertoire. I believe: "Boredom is not a state of mind. Boredom is the state of not using your mind." When you are playful, you can also answer the question, "So, what do you think?" You are willing to contribute your ideas like you did when your kindergarten teacher asked a question and you had to hold your elbow to prevent your raised waving arm from falling off! If you are a student, learn to play in class. Raise your hand. Ask questions. Sit on your knees and hold your elbow! If you are a parent, turn off your kid's TV and pick up a bat and ball. Go for a hike. Teach your kids how to bake a cake. Play a board game under a blanket in your living room. Remember, children will learn by watching your example. If you conduct the dullest staff meetings on the planet, start your next meeting with crayons and coloring books. If you change your approach from boring to *Zing!*, then you change the environmental energy available to others from a negative to a positive!

SKILL BUILDING LESSON

1. Go to Appendix A and complete the self-assessment titled "Playfulness is Serious Business."
2. Hold a bubble gum blowing contest with yourself when no one is watching.
3. Keep a coloring book and crayons in your desk and color when you start to get too serious or stressed.
4. Put colorful and cheerful reminders of your childhood in your environment.
5. Dance. Skip. Jump.
6. Play Simon Says at your next meeting.
7. Read books on creativity. I recommend Doug Hall's *Jump Start Your Brain.*
8. Ask yourself: "Where is the potential for play in this situation?"
9. Carry balloons in your pocket in case of emergencies.

10. During your lunch hour, go to the playground and swing.
11. Begin or revive a hobby.
12. Doodle.
13. Hand out lollypops.
14. Wear a silly hat.
15. Play a practical joke on someone.
16. Hold chair races down the hallway.
17. Try a game of musical chairs before your next committee meeting.
18. While waiting online at the grocery store play "I spy..." with the person behind you.
19. Hang out with kids. Baby-sit your neighbor's kids.
20. Schedule a "Game Night" with friends.

"The secret of genius is the ability to carry the spirit of the child into old age, which means never losing your enthusiasm."
—Aldous Huxley

24

Insight Twenty:
The Gift of Self-Discipline

*"If we are to maintain confidence in ourselves, we must be able to
trust that we will do what we say we are going to do."*
—Sue Patton Thoele

Tom Hanks' portrayal of Forrest Gump won him an Academy
Award. His true reward was how his character inspired a nation. The
writing was so masterful that many of the lines are now part of
American culture, such as: "Stupid is as stupid does" or "Life is like
a box of chocolates..." You can see this movie again and again, each
time catching something you missed in earlier viewings. What fasci-
nates me most about Forrest Gump is his self-discipline. He repeated
specific behaviors despite the required physical, mental, and spiritual effort.

THE DEFINITION OF SELF-DISCIPLINE

Self-discipline is the ability to control or direct yourself for the
sake of becoming a better person or achieving a desired outcome of
self-improvement. Although the word *discipline* can bring about a
negative response, it comes from *disciple* meaning a learner who is
in loving response to a respected teacher. With self-discipline you
are both teacher and student.

Whether your goal is to lose weight, improve your GPA, lower
your golf score, or increase your savings, some degree of regulation
of your energies is required. Nothing is ever accomplished without
a pre-determined direction—or focus—of your efforts. This doesn't
mean you must always know exactly how you want things to turn out;
instead, you know that what you are doing is a step in the right direction.

Self-discipline is attractive because we know first hand how hard it is to achieve on a daily basis. We admire people for their perseverance, endurance, and determination. Self-discipline takes work. It takes sacrifice. Many of us (myself included) just aren't willing to work that hard or give up that much. Often, self-discipline is the difference between those who want and those who get.

THE LOOK OF SELF-DISCIPLINE

We demonstrate self-discipline in a variety of ways as shown below. By contrasting the behaviors of those who have self-discipline against those who don't, you get a clearer picture of how your colleagues, neighbors, employees and friends, draw conclusions about your potential to positively influence them.

SELF-DISCIPLINED	LACKING SELF-DISCIPLINE
Run every day	Drive to the corner store
Carry a bottle of water everywhere	Carry a thermos of coffee everywhere
Snack on an apple	Snack on candy bars
Put yourself in time out	Yell at children
Take a deep breath	Slam doors
Maintain average weight	Maintain obesity
Eat moderate portions	Supersize" all meals
Breathe clean air	Smoke
Manage time	Always frazzled
Drink alcohol in moderation	Binge drink
Finish work on time	Consistently submit late or uncompleted work
Rarely talk about television shows	Discuss soap operas
Make statements, "I abstain from…"	Make statements, "I just can't help myself…"

Which type of characteristics implies an enhanced sense of self-discipline? Which type of characteristics would you trust to accomplish goals, lead you to a greater social good, or make a difference? Although largely surface observations, these characteristics hint at your ability to self-regulate. They may have little to do with your actual competency or abilities, yet have everything to do with how you are received by others.

Moving Forward with Self-Discipline

Forrest Gump liked to run. He didn't always know to where he was running, just that he liked to run. In a classic scene, Forrest sets out running from the West Coast, unsure of his destination. Every time he gets to a new place, he decides to "keep on running." His direction is simply forward. Self-discipline allows you to move forward because you are letting go of self-doubt, insecurity, and the fears associated with change in favor of an internal drive to become someone different—someone better.

I am blessed to work with college students on a regular basis. From new-student orientations to commencement addresses, I observe their successes and failures. By the very act of going to college, they receive more choices and opportunities. Whether you are a returning or part-time student or just out of high school, your pursuit of a degree is a pursuit of self-discipline. This doesn't mean you know which degree you want! This doesn't mean you know what you will do with the degree once you get it, either! But you have put yourself in a position to achieve something—you'll figure out what that is when the time is right. The important thing is to want. Be hungry for a better you. Want a better world.

Components of Self-Discipline

Do you know anyone who makes a statement about what he/she wants, but will never do what it takes to get it? On the other hand, do you know anyone with the ability to discipline his/her life and continually accomplishes his/her goals? People with self-discipline get what they want. Which kind of person would your co-workers, class-mates, friends, and family say you are? The internal commitment to self-discipline begins with an internal decision to either start over or embrace a new way of thinking. You can (and often should) work on a daily basis to build your self-discipline. I recommend the following components as a means of building this skill:

SACRIFICE

What are you prepared to give up? Are you willing to sacrifice time with your family to become the president of your company, or is that too high of a price? Do you have a bad habit like smoking or yelling at your children (or co-workers), but aren't ready to quit? Does the belief "you just don't have any more time" in your day override your desire to make a difference in your community? These are questions of sacrifice. Whether time, money, promotion, affiliation, friends, or favor, what are you willing to give up in pursuit of something greater?

COMMITMENT

Commitment is the ability to establish a sense of loyalty and trustworthiness through a repeated presence and exertion of energy. I like the mental reminders "Are you in or are you out?" or "Jump on board or get off the boat!" In other words, commit fully or admit that the goal isn't really that important to you. Much like you can't be "slightly pregnant," you can't be half-hearted in your desire to make the world a better place. Help out by investing in what matters to you! Do what you can do, but do it fully. Lip service (i.e. "I want to help out, but I can't make it…") is not commitment.

DECISION MAKING

Decision-making is making choices based upon priorities. It's a process of getting rid of the junk in search of the jewels. Have you ever been paralyzed because you have so many options? Picture the process of decision making as a trip to the grocery store. Once you have put everything you want in your cart and make it to check out, you are informed of how much you have to spend! This forces you to put back what you really don't need or can't afford. You must prioritize what is most important to your life so you can avoid doing what doesn't serve that purpose. The key is to simplify and focus. Choose to work on only one or two self-improvement areas at a time. Give them your full attention. Apply a decision you are currently trying to make to the following suggested process:

1. Write down all of your options (i.e. opportunities to make a difference).
2. Re-visit your purpose and philosophy of life statement (found in Appendix A).
3. Cross out those opportunities that don't fit or match up.
4. Examine the feasibility of what remains. Do you have the time, resources, and support, to pursue each option?
5. Identify the remaining items and determine what you need to sacrifice to make a full commitment to each option. Can you afford it?
6. Repeat steps two through five until you have only two options remaining.
7. Discussing these options with others. This practice gives you valuable feedback.
8. Although decision-making experts may use more professional terms... Go with your gut! Choose the one opportunity that feels right to you.

STRUCTURE

If you view self-discipline as a form of self-regulation, it makes sense to organize or make a routine of your behaviors. Individuals with *Zing!* structure their day. They reserve—or devote—certain parts of their day (and week) to the development or commitment of their wellness, spiritual health, family, community, or sense of play. While researching this book, many of the individuals I studied have regular morning workout routines. Many start their day in prayer and devotion before they do anything else. They build their emotional, psychological, and spiritual reserves needed to carry them throughout the day.

HABITS

Make your goals habits! When you make something a habit, you are more inclined to stick with it. Consider the difference between "going on a diet" or "being fit for life." The behaviors are identical; however, the mind set of a "dieter" is that there is a beginning and an end. Fit individuals have integrated working out and eating well into their every day. They "just say no" to Krispy Kreme donuts out of habit. One way to make something a habit is to associate the phrase: "that's just the way it is" with a particular activity.

It's Time for Dinner

My husband and I value family dinner time as a rule, not exception. The kids have a set bedtime. When challenged by competing forces we respond, "because that's just the way it is." In other words, you have to accept the fact that Zing! is about your choices, priorities, and commitments. You may not be the one who schedules gymnastics classes or soccer practice over the dinner hour, but you do get to decide whether or not to register your children for those class times! You get to control your time.

Organization Skills

The last component of self-discipline is the ability to organize your life so as to manage your time. When you are in a complete state of chaos, you send the message that time controls you. Your disorganization translates as poor self-management skills and serves as an individual detractor. Inherent in self-discipline is doing what you need to do to when it ought to be done! I find getting the tasks I don't want to do done first, such as making phone calls, is a form of self-discipline that allows me to get on with my day. Below is a brief look at some of my favorite organizational strategies.

1. Only handle a piece of mail once before acting on it.
2. Open your mail over a garbage can to immediately discard unwanted materials.
3. Set aside the same time every day to make phone calls and return calls.
4. Get your house working for you at the beginning of every day.
5. Never go to bed with dishes in your sink (i.e. no unfinished business).
6. Use bulletin boards for frequently referenced information.
7. Keep the same kind of filing system at home as you would at work.

8.   File—don't pile!
9.   Use your daily planner to forecast time commitments.
10. Create effective systems of organization (i.e. neat, well-labeled storage boxes).
11. Delegate tasks to those more qualified or whose responsibility dictates (i.e. kids clean up their own messes).

Skill-Building Lesson

1.   Go to Appendix A and complete the self-assessment titled "Degrees of Self-Discipline."
2.   Rent *Forrest Gump* and look for signs of self-discipline.
3.   Read the autobiographies of great leaders—their stories contain enormous sacrifice, discipline, and commitment.
4.   Set a small goal with a short deadline. Once you do what you said you would do, increase the goal and increase the deadline.
5.   Enlist someone to check the progress of a goal you've set.
6.   Identify a self-imposed reward for not doing something today you'd normally do.
7.   Identify a self-imposed reward for doing something today you normally wouldn't do.
8.   Make a list of your behaviors that may be perceived as showing a lack of self-discipline.
9.   Keep a record on a highly visible calendar of successful acts of self-discipline.
10. Clearly delineate between a lack of self-discipline and an addiction.
11. If you have one, seek professional assistance for your addiction(s).
12. Make the connection between self-discipline and self-esteem. Do you feel worthy of improvement and making a difference in this world?
13. Start talking about the concept of self-regulation with people in your life and leadership. What have they had to consistently stay away from—or structure into—their lives?

14. Choose one thing that you are going to turn into a routine or habit and do it every day.

> *"To live is so startling it leaves little time for anything else."*
> —Emily Dickinson

25

INSIGHT TWENTY-ONE: THE HAND OF HUMILITY

*"I never did anything alone. Whatever was accomplished in this
country was accomplished collectively."*
—Golda Meir

Remember the Boston Celtics of the Eighties? Larry Bird, Kevin McHale, Bill Walton... now that was a team! They were good. They knew they were good. They played like they knew they were good. Being a Celtic fan (and even if you weren't) you had to admire their skill—they had the talent to back up their confidence. They not only played basketball, they entertained. They played against their opponents both physically and psychologically. The courtside antics, silliness, and intensity made the Boston Garden a magical place. You got caught up in what it felt like to be a winner.

Back then, things like the three-point shooting and slam dunk contests were new. You saw moves you didn't think were possible. One of my favorite memories was watching Larry Bird warm up for the three-point contest without taking off his warm-ups. He didn't miss a shot. When it was time for the actual contest, he still didn't take off his warm-ups. Why should he? He was Larry Bird and he was going to win. He won.

Larry Bird was that good. Despite the fact that a thin line exists between "cockiness" and "confidence," Larry Bird's actions and words happen to be true. According to Charles Spurgeon's definition of humility, speaking the truth is at the core of humility: "*Humility* is to make a right estimate of oneself." However, not too many people can pull off cockiness with style—unless, of course, you played for the Championship Boston Celtics! My rule of thumb is to risk being humble. There's only one Larry Bird.

THE ERA OF HUMILITY

Humility is the "new age" charisma. There is incredible power in giving praise where praise is due, allowing others to shine, and experiencing the personal satisfaction of making the world a better place because you've been here. Reported in the *Harvard Business Review* article "Are You Picking the Right Leaders," researchers James Brant and Melving Sorcher claim: "We have found that many exceptional leaders are modest and display little ambition, even though on the inside they are fiercely competitive. In fact, a high degree of personal humility is far more evident among exceptional leaders than is raw ambition."

When you make humility part of your life and leadership, you literally transform "charisma" from the self-serving "Hey, look at me!" paradigm to "charizma"—with a "z" for *Zing!*. Instead of focusing on what's best for you, you focus on what's best for the greater good. One of the most humble people I have the honor of knowing is Dr. Maureen Hartford, president of Meredith College in Raleigh, North Carolina.

ZING! PROFILE

I met Dr. Hartford over twenty years ago while working at Case Western Reserve University in Ohio. I was right out of graduate school and she was the dean of students. Despite her position of authority over me, I always felt comfortable in her presence. Her style of leadership was to develop the leaders around her. She was available, encouraging, inspiring, and genuinely interested in my life. Since then, I have observed and admired Dr. Hartford's professional advancement, leadership, and work on behalf of advancing opportunities for women.

When asked about her accomplishments, Dr. Hartford responded by quoting Golda Meir (see opening quote). Then she humbly said, "I will tell you about some collective accomplishments." She proudly spoke of hosting one of the first AmeriCorps programs in the country while at the University of Michigan and developing campus-based LeaderShape programs at forty campuses through out the country.

I asked Dr. Hartford to define success. She said, "Success is doing what you enjoy doing and enjoying what you do." I also asked her to define happiness. She responded, "Happiness can come from many sources for me; being with family and friends, meeting new people, having an interesting discussion, reading a book, walking in the sunshine, hugging my cat, meeting a goal I have set, laughing at a good joke, and breaking 90 in golf." She summarized happiness, however, as "balance in my life." Finally, I inquired about her source of strength. She humbly responded, "I find inspiration in each of the women and men I now serve."

LEARNING HUMILITY

Like the other twenty insights, humility can be learned or it may come naturally to you. As a speaker, I find it the hardest insight taught in this book. First, Humility requires honesty—sometimes the painful kind. Secondly, humility isn't easy for a speaker who makes her living on stage or as the center of attention. I've learned, however, one of the best ways to learn about being more humble is to observe (and befriend) influential leaders who demonstrate humility. You can find them if you look hard enough. They are the ones who display the following attributes of humility:

ASK TOUGH QUESTIONS

I frequently have to stop and ask myself: Which direction is my arrow pointing—from me to others or from others to me? Have I been focusing on "what's in it for me?" or "what can I do for you?" By literally replacing your "I" thinking and language with "we" or "you" thinking and language, you will begin to be received as more humble. This technique downplays your own importance.

SERVE OTHERS

Accept your place in the world. If/when you see yourself as a teacher, you will teach. If/when you see yourself as a servant, you will serve with honor. If/when you see yourself as a mentor, you will mentor. Sharing your talents (as opposed to selfishly using them for your own advancement) is an act of humility.

Leadership in the 21st century is not about one person. In fact, I believe today's organizational leader should make themselves replaceable! They should strive to train at least three people who could replace them at any moment. This is way too threatening for the "look at me" kind of charisma, but exactly the kind of "charizmatic" leadership needed to change the world. Shared leadership—while maintaining an articulated vision for all leaders—is the new model of influential leadership. Your willingness to be replaced is a sign of your true worth!

Practice Modesty

Someone once said: *modesty* is the art of drawing attention to whatever it is you are being humble about. You may be the "brains" of your organization, but are you smart enough to give everyone else the credit? Share the praise and look for ways to honor others for their contributions. Whenever possible, avoid self-serving awards and the need to tell others about your latest accomplishments (unless in your inner circle) if it doesn't make them feel better about themselves or serve an inspirational function. If you do find yourself on the receiving end of well wishing individuals, then be grateful and be graceful. Allow the good-doers to praise you, and find a way to maximize your appreciation for their efforts and thoughtfulness. You show grace by deflecting their good wishes towards you back onto them. When accepting praise, remember to keep your remarks brief.

Remain Open for Discussion

Be open to others' thoughts and welcome them. Solicit others' opinions while maintaining the final word. Here's a humbling fact: some people are smarter than you and will have better "wicked-good ideas" than you! Remember to pay special attention to voices of dissension because they will make you think the hardest. 'Yes'-people fill your needs, not those of the greater good. Better yet, surround yourself with great counsel and people who are smarter than you are! Don't be threatened by them; embrace their ideas and knowledge. Learn from them. It takes a great deal of humility to be open for discussion. Others will admire your willingness to be accurate and informed.

Many of my colleagues also struggle with humility. In fact, a fellow speaker recently told me that he doesn't read program evaluations. "Why should I?" he snapped, and cited how many speeches he gives a year, suggesting that his audience members aren't professional speakers and thus don't have a valid opinion. Confidence is essential to a high ZQ, but not when it crosses the line and becomes arrogance. Anytime you have the opportunity to be formally evaluated, take it! How else are you going to know what works and what needs work?

ADMIT MISTAKES

Be willing to admit you made a mistake or were wrong. The world won't come to an end. Everybody makes mistakes because we aren't perfect. That's just the way it is. However, when you do or say something in poor judgment, forget to show up, or fail to prepare as needed, you actually show more humility by admitting your mistake instead of covering it up. Owning your mistakes is significant to *Zing!*; lying and/or blaming others are individual detractors. Failure is not a person; it's a process. You are not a failure; you failed. It's OK to make mistakes. Once you have admitted you erred, you can do something about it. Humility invites you to be human.

People often ask me if saying "I'm sorry" is a sign of weakness. If caring about other human beings is a sign of weakness, then we are all in big trouble! It's worth repeating, saying "I'm sorry" will open more doors than saying "I'm right." Apologizing or asking for forgiveness is a sign of security and strength. It's hard for someone with a lot of ego to admit to being wrong. What's more important to you?

SKILL BUILDING LESSON

1. Go to Appendix A and complete the self-assessment titled "The Art of Humility."
2. Give equal access of your time to everyone.
3. Don't ask someone to do anything you wouldn't do.
4. Take calls without screening them.
5. Share the credit for your success with those who made it possible.
6. Avoid bragging.
7. Talk less about yourself. Be genuinely interested in what

someone else has to say.

8.   Give up your First Class seat to a staff member who never rides in First Class.

9.   Don't assume things are owed to you because of your "status."

10. Stand when others walk into a room.

11. Offer your name in introduction and don't presume others already know it.

12. Move away from behind your desk (a symbol of authority) when talking with others.

13. Share the perks of your position or influence.

14. Pitch in when help is needed, regardless of your job or title.

15. Point out the efforts of others for no apparent reason.

16. To quote Ken Blanchard, "Catch someone doing something right."

"One must become as humble as the dust
before he can discover truth."
—Mahatma Gandhi

26

GIVING TO A GREATER GOOD

"When you make a difference in someone else's life,
your life will be forever different."

To have read this book is to admit your life has meaning, or that you are seeking to give it greater meaning. You do want happiness. You do want to make this world a better place because of your presence on the planet. With this realization comes the conclusion of part one of your journey: you need to believe in yourself before anyone else will believe in you. There is no escaping your call to leadership. You can make a difference. I hope my words have inspired you to act.

Words can do that. They can make you different, especially when you act on them. I first saw the following quote by Dr. Martin Luther King, Jr. on a billboard over twenty years ago: "Anyone can be great because anyone can serve." I had to pull over, write it down, and allow his words to influence my life. It was a gift I didn't need at the time, but later became the answer to many questions about my purpose in life. Whether you accept it or not, you have positive messages of inspiration coming at you all day long. They are there. Do you see them? Even the thoughts you create continue to shape you and your future.

THE FUTURE IS YOURS TO CREATE

You are proof that America in the 21st century isn't void of leadership. It has been re-defined and re-shaped from a search for "heroes" to those who touch our lives daily. From teachers to students, brothers to sisters, parents to children, corporate America to community organizations—you are the future. Once you truly embrace this fact of life, you are in the next part of your journey: shifting the focus of your conversations and efforts from *you* to the collective *we*.

It's time to not only leave your fingerprints wherever you go, it's time to realize your fingerprints will most likely cover up the set left before you arrived. And yours too, will eventually be covered up by someone else's efforts to make the world a better place. It will take a collective effort to make the world a better place. One person can make a difference, but a group of dedicated individuals can work miracles. How can you inspire others to act? Your life is a gift, are you ready to give it to others? Are you ready to love your neighbor's kids like your own, commit to a cause, start a volunteer effort in your company, and encourage others to put into action what they have in their hearts?

THE POSSIBILITIES

Zing! is the means to all these possibilities and more. Why? Because *Zing!* in its purest form is possibility. It is an endless supply of all the things that make our life and leadership possible—including (but not limited to) the twenty-one insights from self-inspection to humility. There is no final chapter when you—and those around you, believe in the possibilities of serving a greater good through a collective effort.

So, what time is it?

IT'S OUR TIME

From the faith of Mother Teresa to the humor of Bob Hope
—it's our time.
From the courage of Gloria Steinhiem to the diligence of Mia Hamm
—it's our time.
From the compassion of Mr. Rogers to the vision of Bill Gates
—it's our time.
From the power of Dr. Martin Luther King to the courage of Rosa Parks
—it's our time.
From the humanity of Jimmy Carter to the persuasiveness of Elizabeth Dole
—it's our time.

From the honor of Sandra Day O'Connor to the magnetism of Oprah Winfrey
—it's our time.
From the optimism of little girls and boys who begin as scouts, to the leader-
ship of men and women who serve as coaches, teachers and community
volunteers
—it's our time.
From the sacrifice of children who take care of their aging parents to the
voices of those who speak up for the homeless
—it's our time.
From the servitude of the men and women fighting in our armed services to
the self-inspection of a nation
—it's our time.
From the young to the old,
From the tall to the short,
From the front row to the back row,
From the right wing to the left wing—and every Zing! in between,
From the opportunity to make a difference in this world to the obligation,
From my words to your meaning,
You—and only you, my friends—will decide how high to climb,
Because now –exclamation point required
—it's our time!

APPENDIX A

CHAPTER SELF-ASSESSMENT OPPORTUNITIES

PRE-TEST
THE PERSONALITY OF INFLUENCE INVENTORY

There are two parts to this inventory: the first part examines how *you* perceive your use of the listed charismatic indicators; the second part examines how *someone else* with whom you interact on a regular basis perceives your use. The results will be more accurate—and helpful—if *both* parts are completed. A POST-TEST is found at the conclusion of this appendix.

Directions: Using the three columns from the left ("Do You?"), place a check-mark under A (Always), S (Sometimes), or N (Never) to indicate the frequency or consistency with which you apply each characteristic of influence. To make this a useful assessment, enlist someone you trust and ask him/her to use the far right three columns ("Does He/She?"), which refers to your characteristics, not theirs.

	Do You?			Does He/She?		
	A	S	N	A	S	N
Characteristics of Influence:						
Exhibit sensitivity to others' needs						
Show appreciation for others' services						
Encourage others to grow						
Compliment others, wanting nothing in return						
Engage others in conversation						
Bring positive energy to projects						
Accurately perceive environmental constraints						
Take personal risks						
Seek opportunities to expand personal skill set						
Handle adversity with grace						
Show consideration towards others						
Effectively express own desires and needs						
Actively listen to the true meaning of a message						
Praise others in public						
Demonstrate acts of kindness						
Possess a well articulated vision of the future						
Read for self-improvement						
Engage in exercise regime						

	A	S	N	A	S	N
Dress appropriately for any given setting						
Incorporate fair play into all interactions						
Count your/his/her blessings						
Remember others' names						
Refrain from finishing others' sentences						
Set high standard of personal conduct						
Cover your/his/her mouth when yawning						
Use proper table manners and table etiquette						
Possess an optimistic outlook on life						
Manage distractions in your/his/ her environment						
Act with modesty						
Exercise self-control						
Use your/his/her time constructively						
Effectively prioritize daily tasks						
Effectively manage your/his/her energy						
Build upon personal strengths						
Keep confidences						
Show gratitude for advantages in life						
Make others feel valued in your/ his/her presence						
Tell the truth at all times						
Create opportunities to network						
Utilize others' talents towards a common goal						
Believe in a greater force other than you/him/her						
Show enthusiasm for life and leadership						
Deal effectively with adversity						
Speak well at the podium or publicly						
Find the humor in difficult situations						

	A	S	N	A	S	N
Possess a sense of playfulness						
Refrain from speaking negatively of others						
Arrive on time to commitments						
Initiate small talk with strangers						
Earn the respect of others						
Nurture others to grow and become better people						
Willingly take self-assessments						
Accept feedback on performance well						
Practice humility and modesty						
Trust others before they give you reason not to						
Possess a strong work ethic						
Encourages others' ideas and involvement						
Possess a network of quality contacts						
Think before speaking						
Make others feel comfortable						

Add column TOTALS: ___ ___ ___ ___ ___ ___

$X2$ $X1$ $X0$ $X2$ $X1$ $X0$

___ + ___ = ___   ___ + ___ = ___

Scoring: Give yourself **2 points** for every *A* response. Give yourself **1 point** for every *S* response and **0 points** for *N* responses. Do this for both your responses and your teammate's. You will end up with two totals. Compare each total with the analysis below, keeping in mind that individual items are not weighed but treated equally. (Note: The more accurate assessment is the one completed by your teammate. Start there.)

If either total is less than 60: You are reading the right book! Pay considerable attention to those factors that influence others' reception of you. Although you may show strength in some characteristics, you should take advantage of all of the skill-building opportunities in this book, including self-assessments. You are encouraged to discuss with your teammate, his or her responses.

If either total is between 61 and 100: You are still reading the right book! Pay attention to whether you scored closer to 61 or closer to 100. The range accounts for the fact that others' perceptions may have more or less significance, depending upon the nature of your relationship and the extent to which they are able to observe all of the listed traits. This score suggests you actively work on improving your skill sets and have an interest in being happier. For best results, seek out the insights and accompanying skill building lessons in each chapter. Focus on one insight a week. Practice makes perfect!

If either total is over 100: *Zing!* is your thing! Your ability to influence others is quite high. Still, attend to those traits to which your teammate responded with *S* or *N*, even if you disagree with him/her. Do you see a common factor or pattern among those responses? Is it possible you don't practice those traits on a regular basis?

INSIGHT ONE:
ON SELF-ASSESSMENT

Directions: Answer T for True, F for False, or U for Unsure, to the following questions under the appropriate column.

	T	F	U
I am confident in my abilities.			
I am not open to feedback about my skills.			
I effectively give feedback to others regarding their skills.			
I rarely take time to examine my own weaknesses.			
I actively seek self-improvement opportunities.			
When criticized, I blame someone or something else.			
I have created space in my life for self-reflection.			
I am afraid of what self-examination will tell me.			
I find growth potential in hearing others' opinions of my skills.			
I am perfect – just the way I am.			

Scoring: For the odd statements marked True, give yourself 1 point. For the even statements marked False, give yourself 1 point. For statements marked Unsure, give yourself 0 points.

If you scored 7 or higher: you already practice self-examination and know its usefulness.

If you scored 6 or below: take time to ask yourself why you are uncomfortable with self-examination. What threatens you?

INSIGHT TWO:
YOUR CONTENT OF CHARACTER – IN A WORD

Directions: To quickly access your content of character think of the *one* word that would describe your entire being, if you could only describe it in one word. Consider if that's the same word others would choose for you. Here are some possibilities:

> Truthful or dishonest?
> Happy or sad?
> Energizer or slacker?
> Parent or professional?
> Giver or taker?
> Determined or unmotivated?
> Helper or self-focused?
> Possessive or independent?
> Achiever or underachiever?

Now, review the extensive list of values on the next page. Place a check mark next to the ones that matter to your life and leadership. Then, go back and select the three values most important to you. This is harder than it appears. Your life and leadership should be guided by your top three values. If they're not, spend time identifying where the disconnect occurs. What do you need to do to walk the walk and talk the talk?

Achievement	Imagination	Strength
Action	Individuality	Success
Beauty	Intelligence	Talent
Bravery	Justice	Thinking
Career	Kindness	Tolerance
Change	Leadership	Trust
Charity	Learning	Truth
Children	Life	Understanding
Common Sense	Love	Values
Confidence	Loyalty	Virtue
Conscience	Marriage	Wealth
Contentment	Money	Winning
Courage	Morals	Wisdom
Curiosity	Obligation	Wit
Dignity	Passion	Work
Education	Patience	Youth
Enjoyment	Patriotism	Zeal
Equality	Peace	
Excellence	Perfection	
Experience	Perseverance	
Faith	Philanthropy	
Family	Planning	
Forgiveness	Politeness	
Freedom	Power	
Friendship	Praise	
Generosity	Pride	
Giving	Progress	
Goals	Purpose	
Gratitude	Quality	
Greatness	Reason	
Growth	Reputation	
Happiness	Respect	
Health	Responsibility	
Honesty	Security	
Hope	Service	
Humility	Simplicity	
Humor	Solitude	
Ideals	Spiritual	

INSIGHT THREE:
LIFE MISSION STATEMENT

How you define life dictates how you live your life.

Directions: Using the space provided below write your life philosophy statement by completing each sentence. Before you begin, think about the values that are important to you (refer to values list from the previous assessment.) Consider what inspires your life and leadership.

Life is...

_____

_____

_____

_____

_____

What is important to me is...

_____

_____

_____

_____

_____

Therefore, I choose to live my life by...

_____

_____

_____

_____

_____

INSIGHT FOUR:
MAKING VISION A REALITY

Directions: Answer (T) for true or (F) for false to the following statements.

	T	F
I provide others with a sense of security.		
There is always a better way or more than one way to get things done.		
I am a "big picture" thinker. I see what others can't see.		
My ideas surprise others.		
People ask me, "What do you think?" on a regular basis.		
I freely share my creative thoughts.		
Others look to me for direction.		
I give advice freely.		
I often have already thought of an idea before someone else brings it up.		
I am clear about the direction of my life.		
I am clear about the direction of my career or vocation.		
I effectively lead others towards a shared vision.		
I frequently receive positive feedback for my thinking outside of the box.		
I often seek new ways of achieving my goals.		
Others can easily see and describe what I value.		
I am willing to risk being criticized for having a vision.		
I am not afraid to say what I think in a group.		
I frequently have a different opinion than others in my group.		
I know I will do great things with my life and leadership.		
Others' opinions belong to them.		

Score: The statements above reflect your vision of life and leadership. Count the number of TRUE responses.

Number True: ____ ____

15 TRUE: You are clearly a visionary thinker. Others recognize you as such and look to you for guidance. Remember that the ability to articulate a vision is not a common trait; therefore, people will respect you for not going along with the majority opinion.

10 to 14 TRUE: You are a team player and don't like to go against the majority opinion for fear of making more work for yourself, being wrong, rejected, fired, etc. Be careful about confusing consensus building with good decision making! The charismatic leader is always willing to verbalize in a clear, straightforward fashion, when a group is moving forward and when the group has strayed off course. Don't be afraid to risk being right! Take more chances.

9 or below TRUE: Stop and ask yourself if you know where you want your life and leadership to go. Ask yourself if you clearly understand where your involvements, responsibilities, and obligations, *are* going. In order to have *Zing!*, you need answers to these questions. (You are reading the right book.)

INSIGHT FIVE:
PICTURE THIS

Directions: Sit back in your chair. Relax. In this order, review the following:

Consider the one thing in life that scares you the most.
What specifically scares you about this one thing?
Why are you afraid of this?
If this fear became a reality, what is the worst thing that could happen?
How do you know?
Has anything in your life caused you to feel this about this outcome?
What would it take to confront this fear and move on?
Answer yes or no. Are you willing to try?

Process: Repeat this series of questions (in order) using a variety of situations. With each question, you dig deeper into your real fears. To simply say, "I'm afraid to speak in public" may mask deeper fears of rejection. Is it possible you are afraid of rejection because you are afraid of being alone or, because you really don't enjoy your own company? Every question takes you to a greater understanding. The goal of this exercise is to explore mastering more productive skill sets.

INSIGHT SIX:
THE ADVERSITY IN MY LIFE AND LEADERSHIP

Directions: Using the Response to Adversity chart below, consider examples and situations in your life and leadership that represent sources of adversity. Write each situation in the appropriate box. Consider how you responded. In each box under "Better Response," write about how a different reaction might have served you better.

	IN YOUR CONTROL *(CHOICES YOU MAKE)*	**OUT OF YOUR CONTROL** *(LIFE)*
Past	*Your situation:* *How you responded:* *How you could have responded:*	*Your situation:* *How you responded:* *How you could have responded:*
Present	*Your situation:* *How you responded:* *How you could have responded:*	*Your situation:* *How you responded:* *How you could have responded:*

TIME FRAME

INSIGHT SEVEN:
THEN AND NOW EXERCISE

Directions: In the spaces provided and under the proper headings describe yourself at that time period. Be specific. List your interests, activities, goals etc. If you are old enough, go back ten years and twenty years as well. *Today* is the comparative measure. When you are done filling in the boxes, consider crossing out an entire line. How would your life and leadership be different?

Today:
_____
_____
_____
_____
_____

Five years ago:
_____
_____
_____
_____
_____

Ten years ago:
_____
_____
_____
_____
_____

Twenty years ago:
_____
_____
_____
_____
_____

Process: There is always a reason why you became who you are or did what you did. Consider the value of things you did for no apparent reason at all. Where they good decisions? Use the space below to record the motivation behind your actions today, five years ago, ten and so on:

Today:
_____
_____
_____
_____
_____

Five years ago:
_____
_____
_____
_____

Ten years ago:
_____
_____
_____
_____

Twenty years ago:
_____
_____
_____
_____

INSIGHT EIGHT:
A MATTER OF ATTITUDE

Your attitude goes where you go. Is it heavy or light to carry around? There aren't many things in this world that are 100% under your control, but your attitude is one thing you get to decide.

Directions: Next to each characteristic listed below, place a T for True or an F for False indicating if you possess that characteristic a majority of the time.

Do YOU…

1. _____ *Think about how to reach your goals.*
2. _____ *Point out others' faults.*
3. _____ *Speak negatively about yourself.*
4. _____ *Think that every day is a new day.*
5. _____ *Marvel at the stupidity surrounding you.*
6. _____ *Believe in your potential.*
7. _____ *Dislike being asked, "How are you?"*
      because the person asking really doesn't care.
8. _____ *Question why someone is being nice to you.*
9. _____ *Offer to help others.*
10. _____ *Notice the goodness in others.*
11. _____ *Often wonder, "What's in this for me?"*
12. _____ *Know that when something breaks, it can usually be fixed.*
13. _____ *Take responsibility for your state of mind.*
14. _____ *Ask complete strangers, "How are you?" then listen to what they say.*
15. _____ *Believe others are waiting for you to fail so they can point it out to you.*
16. _____ *Would send yourself flowers if no one else*
      was going to and you wanted flowers.
17. _____ *Have no goals or dreams because they won't ever come true.*
18. _____ *Blame others for the way you get treated by them.*
19. _____ *Value the day.*
20. _____ *Would never want a friend to send you a small gift.*
21. _____ *Live for 5pm, weekends and vacations.*
22. _____ *Think you have high self-esteem.*
23._____ *See little meaning in what you do.*

24. _____ *Think motivational books are pointless.*
25. _____ *Laugh at your own stupidity.*
26. _____ *Think about ways to motivate yourself from the inside out.*

Scoring:
Row 1: Circle which statements above you marked false: 2, 3, 5, 7, 8, 11, 15, 17, 18, 20, 21, 23, 24
Row 2: Circle which statements above you marked true: 1, 4, 6, 9, 10, 12, 13, 14, 16, 19, 22, 25, 26

Record the amount of numbers circled in Row 1 = _____
Record the amount of numbers circles in Row 2 = _____
Add both rows to achieve your TOTAL SCORE: _____

Interpreting Your Total Score:

If your total score is between 22-26: This score suggests a very upbeat and positive attitude about life in general. You enjoy people and your perception of your environment reflects a high level of self-esteem. You have what it takes to achieve any of your goals and work effectively with others – all YOU have to do is make the effort! Change only happens when you act. Your attitude is a "Can Do" attitude.

If your total score is between 14-22: This score suggests there's room for improvement. You are still relying on external sources of motivation as a means of making yourself happy. Work on owning your own perceptions. Try not to see the glass is half empty but focus (via thinking) on finding a water fountain. Don't be afraid to treat yourself better. Keep cleaning the lens you use to view life by looking for the small pleasures and gifts. There is plenty of room for a more productive attitude. Look inward. Trust your potential.

If your total score is between 0-13: This score suggests a significant amount of negativity in your perception of life. Until you change the way you look at your environment, your glass will always be half empty. Remember, the energy you put out there is the energy you get to draw from! You do care about you – or you wouldn't be reading this book! Believe you deserve happiness.

INSIGHT NINE:
PRAISE PREPARATION

Directions: Identify one person you call a friend, one person who has authority over you, and someone you have authority over. Using each method of praise identified below, list specific ideas on how you can expand your influence with each person through your actions:

	PERSON 1	*PERSON 2*	*PERSON 3*
	_____	_____	_____

TYPES OF PRAISE

Recognition	_____	_____	_____
	_____	_____	_____
	_____	_____	_____
	_____	_____	_____

Attention   _____   _____   _____

                     _____   _____   _____

                     _____   _____   _____

                     _____   _____   _____

*Compensation*_____   _____   _____

                     _____   _____   _____

                     _____   _____   _____

                     _____   _____   _____

Evaluation   _____   _____   _____

                     _____   _____   _____

                     _____   _____   _____

                     _____   _____   _____

INSIGHT TEN:
RESPECT

Directions: Identify one person who would perceive *you* as showing him/her little to no respect.

Step One. Write name here: _____.

Step Two. How do you demonstrate that you don't respect him/her?

_____

_____

_____

_____

_____

_____

_____

_____

Step Three. Choose two of the behaviors above. Spend one week devoted to improving one of those behaviors. Use the second week to continue improving the first behavior while working to improve the second behavior.

Step Four. Return to this page and record if you have noticed a difference in how this person is responding to you. Has his/her interaction with you changed as a result of your change of behavior with him/her?

_____

_____

_____

_____

_____

_____

_____

_____

_____

Step Five. Staying with this same individual, go back to step two. Take another behavior from your list and repeat the process. If needed, try additional behaviors or identify more people to respect and practice these steps with them. You may trip and fall, but your efforts will pay off.

INSIGHT ELEVEN
FIT TO LIVE AND FIT TO LEAD

Directions: Using the spaces provided, write (T) for true and (F) for false to indicate whether you engage in these practices a majority of the time. If you are having difficulty determining what constitutes "a majority" of the time, you probably do not engage in the practice enough or often. Therefore, respond with an F.

_____ *I wake up rested.*

_____ *I have a best friend.*

_____ *I eat a healthy breakfast.*

_____ *I challenge my intellect to learn more.*

_____ *I use stairs instead of an elevator.*

_____ *I know how to prepare healthy meals.*

_____ *I am my ideal weight, or am working to reach it.*

_____ *I brush my teeth at least twice a day.*

_____ *I floss daily.*

_____ *I go to annual dental check-ups.*

_____ *I go to annual physical.*

_____ *I have annual eye exams*

_____ *I lift weights three times a week.*

_____ *I drink at least eight glasses of water a day.*

_____ *I do not smoke or inhale secondhand smoke.*

_____ *I never drive after drinking.*

_____ *I drink in moderation (less than three glasses*
      of wine or three beers per week).

_____ *I drive within the speed limit.*

_____ *I practice a faith that sustains me.*

_____ *I know someone who I can contact when I need to talk.*

_____ *I sleep at least seven hours a night.*

_____ *I eat three servings of fruits a day.*

_____ I don't take risks with my health.

_____ I feel energized and healthy.

_____ I stretch at least three times a week.

_____ I take a daily vitamin(s).

_____ I manage my anger.

_____ I expend/conserve enough emotional and
psychological energy to manage my day.

_____ I wear a seatbelt in a car.

_____ I practice "safe" interpersonal relations.

_____ I maintain relationships based upon mutual respect.

_____ My memory seldom fails me.

_____ I am not involved in "dysfunctional" relationships.

_____ I possess internal strength.

_____ I am capable of rational thinking.

_____ I can control my emotions.
_____ I maintain my mental, physical, spiritual, and emotional health.

Scoring: Depending upon which answers were false, your risk level could be significantly higher than having a certain number of false responses. Therefore, no scoring is provided. You are encouraged to review the responses marked false and take steps to improve those areas. Use the space below to record how you feel about your fitness.

_____

_____

_____

_____

_____

_____

_____

_____

INSIGHT TWELVE: IN MY MIND

The traits of intelligence from Chapter 16 are listed below. Instead of relying on the obvious indicators (such as career path or position within a company), use this list to step outside of yourself and consider what you communicate to others about your level of intelligence. Do others see you as smart? Do you take advantage of opportunities to pursue greater knowledge and intellectual stimulation?

Directions: Under the appropriate column, mark (+) for *positive*, (-) for *negative* or (N) for *neutral*, to represent the contribution each trait makes to your overall intellectual perception. Note: Your actual intelligence is not being evaluated. Your goal is to assess if you are maximizing opportunities for your intellectual development.

Trait of Intelligence Indicator:

_____

(+)   (N)   (-)

_____ *The books you read.*

_____ *The content of your conversations including vocabulary and grammar.*

_____ *Teaching others.*

_____ *The media you expose yourself to.*

_____ *Associations with intelligent people.*

_____ *Knowledge of current world affairs.*

_____ *The ability to grasp new ideas and respond to them (i.e. adaptability).*

_____ *Your participation in conversations.*

_____ *Your open-mindedness.*

_____ *Frequency and types of questions you ask.*

____ *Frequency of inaccurate statements you try to present as truth.*

____ *Your conduct in class or meetings.*

____ *Your ability to recall information.*

____ *The degree to which you appreciate the arts and*
        support cultural enhancement.

Scoring: Add up the number of traits that were (+) *positive*, (-) *negative* or (N) *neutral*, and place that number below.

_____ _____ _____   *Totals*
(+)   (N)   (-)

Process: Are you missing opportunities to develop intellectually? If you had more negative or neutral responses than positive responses, consider the magnet pull of your intelligence is not favorable. If the reverse is true, you are sending a more positive message about the significance you place on knowledge acquisition and intelligence.

INSIGHT THIRTEEN:
DETERMINED

What do you really want in life and why aren't you risking your life to save it? Risk is an important component in goal obtainment. The old saying "No pain, no gain" holds true. When faced with making decisions, you are encouraged to ask yourself, "What's the worst thing that could happen?" Aside from doing harm to others, or dying, have you actually considered a dream you have and the reasons why you are not actively pursuing it? Here's your chance.

Directions: On a blank sheet of paper, write down one of your dreams or wishes in life. Underneath, write down why it would be wonderful to get what you want. On the remainder of the page, write down all the reasons why you can't have what you want. Go nuts! After your page is full, examine every reason. Turn the sheet over and on the top write "What's the worst thing that could realistically happen?" Now, fill your sheet again. Examine your responses. Next to each response, write down "But, I could..." and fill in the blank. Your goal is to see how many reasons why not to do something are actually not reasons at all.

INSIGHT FOURTEEN:
THE ART OF COMMUNICATING

Like previous assessments, this one also requires another person's opinion of your skill level. Not only does this keep you honest, but it allows you to see how you are received by others.

Directions: Under column (A), check off whether you practice a particular skill; A = always, S = Sometimes, or N = Never. Then, invite someone who knows you to complete the assessment about how effectively you practice each trait under column (B) Does He/She?

Do You...

	(A) Do YOU?			(B) Does He/She?		
	A	S	N	A	S	N
Hear what isn't being said?						
Listen to the emotion behind words?						
Maintain eye-contact during conversations?						
Paraphrase (repeat comment to person in own words)?						
Make strangers comfortable with small talk?						
Confront in private?						
Manage your emotions during confrontation?						
Change others' behaviors through confrontation?						
Follow up when you say you'll follow up?						
Write clearly?						
Possess a growing vocabulary?						
Sound intelligent?						
Use grammar correctly						
Match your words to your body language?						
Refrain from speaking over someone else's words?						
Let silence happen?						
Rearrange a room so people can network better?						
Sit when talking to someone of a different height?						

	(A) Do YOU?			(B) Does He/She?		
	A	S	N	A	S	N
Refrain from raising your voice in disagreement?						
Express your thoughts accurately?						
Challenge inappropriate remarks?						
Stand when meeting someone?						
Stand up for your own rights to an opinion?						
Protect others' rights to disagree with you?						
Control for various types of "noise" in conversations?						

INSIGHT FIFTEEN:
WHAT DID YOU HEAR?

Directions: Read the scenarios below. The speaker uses the same words in all three examples, but each has a completely different meaning. To identify the statement's true meaning, you must accurately read the provided clues. Circle the letter that best represents what you heard.

Scenario 1. A colleague walks up to you and says, "I quit. That's it." She then puts her head in her hands. Her shoulders drop. She sighs.

What did you hear?

a. She is going to resign.   b. She is frustrated.   c. She did something stupid.

Scenario 2. A colleague walks up to you and says, "I quit. That's it." She has a smirk on her face and swings her head backwards. She rolls her eyes.

What did you hear?

a. She is going to resign.   b. She is frustrated.   c. She did something stupid.

Scenario 3. A colleague walks up to you and says, "I quit. That's it." She avoids eye contact with you. She turns and walks away.

What did you hear?

a. She is going to resign.   b. She is frustrated.   c. She did something stupid.

Process: Scenario 1 is about frustration (b) – you know this because she implies an absence of total defeat signified by hands over her face and her sitting to continue the dialogue. She isn't finished.

In Scenario 3, she walks away without leaving opportunity to change her mind and the lack of eye-contact supports the escaping body language (a).

In Scenario 2, your colleague made the statement as a protective mechanism. If she quits, she can't get fired. However, the smirk and playful toss of the head implies a willingness to work through her stupid move.

INSIGHT SIXTEEN:
PUBLIC SPEAKING HOMEWORK

Use the following questions to evaluate someone else's speaking abilities. After you have done this, give these questions to someone who can evaluate your speaking abilities.

Directions: Place a check mark next to each trait whenever it is used (under "Frequency of Use" column).

Trait:	Frequency of Use					
Compliments audience						
Smiles						
Laughs at self						
Expresses appreciation to the audience						
Lets silence happen						
Asks a question and listens to the answer						
Interacts with audience prior to taking the podium						
Leaves the podium during speech						
Uses a personal story to make a point						
Quotes someone famous						
Tells an appropriate joke						
Changes course when audience isn't reacting						
Uses PowerPoint presentation as a back-up of major points						
Identifies five or less major points						
Uses another medium to make or support a point						
Visually demonstrates or supports a point						
Uses hand gestures						
If he/she strays from outline gets back on track						
References additional sources of information						
Faces right, left, and center audience equally						
Let's go of material not covered if running out of time						
Appears to be having fun						
Handles difficult questions appropriately						

Admits to not knowing an answer					
Clarifies a question if no one responds					
Uses silence effectively					
Makes sexist, oppressive, or defensive remarks					
Makes a self-serving comment (speaks out of ego)					
Apologizes for being "bad" or not knowing something					
Points out when he/she has lost his/her place					
Uses a distracting body movement or word (i.e. "um")					
Uses sarcasm to make a point					

GRADE THE SPEAKER:

a. On a scale of 1 (awful) to 10 (exceptional) how did this presentation rate in your eyes? _____

b. On a scale of 1 (insignificant) to 10 (worthy) how did this speaker make you feel? _____

FOLLOW UP QUESTIONS:

How would you describe the speaker's perceptiveness to his/her audience?

What methods did the speaker use to engage his/her audience?

How did the speaker respond if the audience appeared to not respond?

What various methods of instruction were used to make points?

What five or less points were made?

How effectively was the speaker's content presented?

How well did the speaker use visual aids?

How did the speaker handle questions?

What did the speaker do to persuade the audience to listen to his/her point of view?

What did the speaker do to demonstrate his/her confidence?

INSIGHT SEVENTEEN:
RELATIONSHIP POTENTIAL 101

Directions: Using the sliding scale provided, mark the point that best indicates the frequency of occurrence for each question.

	0%	25%	50%	75%	100%
	FREQUENCY SCALE				
I like hanging out with me.					
I like to working for me.					
I would want to be in a friendship with me.					
I would date me – or marry me.					
I don't make people feel invisible.					
I am open-minded to others' ideas.					
I can be trusted to keep confidences.					
I am attentive in conversations.					
I actively engage in conversations.					
I check my ego at the door.					
My social group is admirable.					
I respect my friends.					
I respect my co-workers.					
I create mutually beneficial relationships.					
I give out business cards.					
I rely on an inner circle.					
I remember names following introductions.					
I shake hands while standing.					
I shake hands during introductions.					
I shake hands after a conversation or greeting.					

	0%	25%	50%	75%	100%
I thank people and "pay it forward."					
I practice talking to strangers.					
I "check in" with people.					
I nurture my relationships.					

Process: To assist you in seeing your perceptions of your relationship building skills, connect the marks on your frequency scale. Are you "all over the place" or are you rather consist in the effort you make to connect with others? Which series of questions appear to be your weak areas? In a week, re-take this assessment using a different colored pen. Look at your improvement!

INSIGHT EIGHTEEN:
A PUNCH OF HUMOR

Comedian Steve Allen notes that laughter is contagious. He contends, as I do, that when you get people laughing, they are more inclined to continue laughing. Think of the last time you thought something was really funny. I mean, your sides hurt because you were laughing so hard. You had tears coming down your cheeks and your last comment was, "I can't remember the last time I laughed this hard!" Close your eyes and visualize the situation. After you have replayed every aspect of the situation, ask yourself, Why it was so funny? What components of what makes people laugh were at play or work? Pay attention to the elements of humor you use as you engage in conversations. What make them laugh? What makes you laugh?

INSIGHT NINETEEN:
PLAYFULNESS IS SERIOUS BUSINESS

The following scenarios offer an opportunity for you to practice playful approaches to challenging situations. Your goal is to identify the response—or create one—that offers the benefits of playfulness, curiosity, and fun.

Directions: Select the answer that best characterizes your understanding and application of playfulness.

Your friend informs you that he/she is considering running for the local school board. You...

_____ *Send him/her an inspiring card.*

_____ *Send an email of congratulations.*

_____ *Wrap up an old pair of sneakers and send with a note, "Thought you might need these!"*

_____ *Take him/her out for lunch.*

_____

You have to work late, along with other colleagues, to meet a deadline. No one is particularly happy about the situation. You...

_____ *Refrain from complaining.*

_____ *Go into your office and close the door to concentrate.*

_____ *Skip dinner.*

_____ *Tell everyone there will be a fifteen minute pizza party in your office at 8pm – they bring the drinks, you'll order the pizza.*

_____

You need to send your clients – or those you associate with professionally – some form of appreciation for their loyalty and business. You…

____ Send them an email of appreciation.

____ Send flowers and/or candy.

____ Send two coffee mugs, gift certificate for coffee, and a note, "Next time, I'll come in person."

____ Call them.

_____

You are in a conversation with someone who is going on and on about absolutely nothing and you have to get going. You…

____ Stand there nodding patiently.

____ Ask the person if you can hug them.

____ Look at your watch.

____ Tell them you have to leave.

_____

Someone has had good news – or reason to celebrate. You…

____ Fill his/her office (or car) with balloons.

____ Send a congratulations card.

____ Take him/her out for lunch.

____ Sing "Happy Birthday!" or an appropriate song.

_____

Someone seated next to you on a plane takes off his/her shoes. Their feet stink. Your eyes are watering. You…

_____ *Sit there and cry.*

_____ *Hit your call button.*

_____ *Smile and say, "OK, this means war. I'm going to take off my shoes, too!"*

_____ *Put a blanket over your head.*

_____

You are having a really bad day. You arrive home to a messy house. You…

_____ *Blast your favorite CD pick up as you move to the music.*

_____ *Yell at your kids, cat, or dog.*

_____ *Throw everyone's clothes out the window (in honor of my mother's approach).*

_____ *Angrily pick up the mess.*

_____

You are delayed in an airport for five hours with strangers. You…

_____ *Find the closest bar.*

_____ *Ask for the Customer Service phone number to complain.*

_____ *Play Hearts on your computer for five hours.*

_____ *Find the closest kid and see if he/she will play tic-tac-toe with you.*

_____

You have volunteered to substitute teach and walk into a room of less than motivated tenth graders just looking to make your day bad. You…

_____ *Challenge them to a game of Simon Says.*

_____ *Tell them to sit down and shut up.*

_____ *Hide behind the desk and look busy.*

_____ *Pray.*

_____

*Your dry cleaners don't have your clothes back when they said they would.
You…*

_____ *Tell them you will never use their services again.*

_____ *Slam the door on your way out.*

_____ *Show them your receipt highlighting the due date.*

_____ *Smile and say, "How about a Big Mac and fries?"*

_____

Process: My point is that you can change the outcome of situations by taking things less seriously. You will either make a situation better or worse by the type of energy you bring to it. Look for the humor, fun, and chance to play with people of all ages. The responses I intended to be playful include: 1.c 2. d 3. c. 4. b 5. a 6. c 7. a 8. d 9. a 10. d

How did you do? If you chose the playful responses, you get my message. If not, it's time to get silly!

INSIGHT TWENTY:
DEGREES OF SELF-DISCIPLINE

Directions: Take a moment to answer the questions below. After you have responded, consider a response fitting of someone with *Zing!*. At this point, you know what it takes. Do you have it?

How would you describe your ability to do tasks you don't want to do?

Who is the most self-disciplined person you know? Why do you identify him/her as self-disciplined?

What challenge(s) have you face regarding self-discipline? From where did you find your strength?

What would you like to accomplish, but haven't because you've lacked the ability to regulate your actions?

How might you begin to take steps to gain more control of your actions to accomplish a goal? What can serve as an external deadline?

What can you do on a regular basis that would turn a desired behavior into a habit?

As a result of reading this chapter, what do you need to change?

INSIGHT TWENTY-ONE:
THE ART OF HUMILITY

Directions: Make a list of five acts of humility you have witnessed and who performed them. Describe how or why each act of humility meets any or all of the five components listed in Chapter 25: Asking Tough Questions, Servitude, Modesty, Open for Discussion, and Admitting Your Mistakes.

ACT OF HUMILITY: *PERFORMED BY:*

1. _____

_____

_____

2. _____

_____

_____

3. _____

_____

_____

4. _____

_____

_____

5. _____

_____

_____

What can you conclude? Which traits clearly demonstrated another person's sense of humility and humbleness? Remember that these are traits that *you* found significant. Which of the above traits do you possess?

POST-TEST

THE PERSONALITY OF INFLUENCE INVENTORY

Now that you have completed this book and have started to apply various insights, it's time to see if your work is paying off. As a reminder, there are two parts to this inventory: the first part examines how *you* perceive your use of the listed charismatic indicators; the second part examines how *someone else* with whom you interact on a regular basis perceives your use. The results will be more accurate—and helpful—if *both* parts are completed.

Directions: Using the three columns from the left ("Do You?"), place a check-mark under *A* (Always), *S* (Sometimes), or *N* (Never) to indicate the frequency or consistency with which you apply each characteristic of influence. To make this a useful assessment, enlist someone you trust and ask him/her to use the far right three columns ("Does He/She?"), which refers to *your* characteristics, not theirs.

	Do You?			Does He/She?		
Characteristics of Influence:	*A*	*S*	*N*	*A*	*S*	*N*
Exhibit sensitivity to others' needs						
Show appreciation for others' services						
Encourage others to grow						
Compliment others, wanting nothing in return						
Engage others in conversation						
Bring positive energy to projects						
Accurately perceive environmental constraints						
Take personal risks						
Seek opportunities to expand personal skill set						
Handle adversity with grace						
Show consideration towards others						
Effectively express own desires and needs						

	A	S	N	A	S	N
Actively listen to the true meaning of a message						
Praise others in public						
Demonstrate acts of kindness						
Possess a well articulated vision of the future						
Read for self-improvement						
Engage in exercise regime						
Dress appropriately for any given setting						
Incorporate fair play into all interactions						
Count your/his/her blessings						
Remember others' names						
Refrain from finishing others' sentences						
Set high standard of personal conduct						
Cover your/his/her mouth when yawning						
Use proper table manners and table etiquette						
Possess an optimistic outlook on life						
Manage distractions in your/his/her environment						
Act with modesty						
Exercise self-control						
Use your/his/her time constructively						
Effectively prioritize daily tasks						
Effectively manage your/his/her energy						
Build upon personal strengths						
Keep confidences						
Show gratitude for advantages in life						
Make others feel valued in your/his/her presence						
Tell the truth at all times						
Create opportunities to network						
Utilize others' talents towards a common goal						
Believe in a greater force other than you/him/her						
Show enthusiasm for life and leadership						
Deal effectively with adversity						

	A	S	N	A	S	N
Speak well at the podium or publicly						
Find the humor in difficult situations						
Possess a sense of playfulness						
Refrain from speaking negatively of others						
Arrive on time to commitments						
Initiate small talk with strangers						
Earn the respect of others						
Nurture others to grow and become better people						
Willingly takes self-assessments						
Accept feedback on performance well						
Practice humility and modesty						
Trust in others before they give you reason not to						
Possess a strong work ethic						
Encourages others' ideas and involvement						
Possess a network of quality contacts						
Think before speaking						
Make others feel comfortable						

Add column TOTALS: __ __ __ __ __ __

X 2 X1 X0 X2 X1 X0

__ + __ = __   __ + __ = __

Scoring: Give yourself **2 points** for every *A* response. Give yourself **1 point** for every *S* response and **0 points** for *N* responses. Do this for both your responses and your teammate's. You will end up with two totals. Compare each total with the totals in your PRE-TEST at the beginning of the appendix. Have you been making improvements? Do you *Zing!* more? (I'm sure you do.) Congratulations on your efforts.

APPENDIX B

COMMUNITY OPPORTUNITIES AND RESOURCES

THE BIG BROTHERS BIG SISTERS PROGRAM
OF GREATER NEW BEDFORD, MA

The Big Brothers Big Sisters Program, a component of Child and Family Services, is a nationally recognized mentor program that has been serving millions of children since 1904. Big Brothers Big Sisters of Greater New Bedford, MA is committed to improving the lives of children by matching them with one to one supported relationships with adult volunteers. Volunteers range in age from 17 to retirement with diverse social, economic, and cultural backgrounds. The children benefit from the program by having someone special to spend time with and enjoy. As a result, their self esteem and school performance are enhanced. Specifically, children with mentors are 52% less likely to skip a day of school, 33% less likely to become involved in violence, and 46% less likely to start using drugs.

Consider becoming a volunteer in your local community or help support the children in New Bedford, MA by sending a financial donation to Child and Family Services of New Bedford, Big Brother Big Sister Program, 800 Purchase Street, New Bedford, MA 02740. For more information contact: 508-990-0894.

EDWARD L URBANOWSKI MEMORIAL FUND

The Eddie L. Urbanowski Memorial Fund was established by his family to assist other families in covering non-reimbursable expenses associated with caring for their children undergoing cancer treatment. Currently, the fund is being used to assist in parking fees at UMASS Memorial Hospital in Worcester, MA. Edward L. Urbanowski (Eddie) died on October 26, 2003 after a four year battle with Leukemia. He was twelve years old. Donations can be made in his name to: Barre Savings Bank, Pleasant Street, Paxton, MA 01612. To reach the bank directly, call: 508-799-2274.

ALTERNATIVES IN MOTION

Founded by author, speaker and friend, Johnnie Tuitel in 1995, Alternatives in Motion is based upon the belief everyone should have the opportunity to participate in society and not be hindered by mobility issues. Alternatives in Motion provides wheelchairs to people who need them but cannot afford them, and don't qualify for any other financial assistance. You can help by volunteering, donating a wheelchair or making a financial contribution. To learn more about how you can make a difference, visit: www.alternativesinmotion.org or contact George Ranville at 877-468-9335. Donations can be sent directly to: Alternatives in Motion, 1916 Bretown South East, Grand Rapids, MI 49506.

NOTES

CHAPTER 1

1. Rakesh Khurana, "The Curse of the Superstar CEO," *Harvard Business Review*, September 2002, 60.
2. Ibid.
3. Jay A. Conger, Rabindra N. Kanungo, and Sanjay T. Menon, "Charismatic leadership and follower effects," *Journal of Organizational Behavior*, **21**, 2000, 747-767.
4. Ibid. The Conger-Kanungo charismatic leadership scale has been found to have sound psycho-metiric properties with reliability and convergent and discriminant validity coefficients.

CHAPTER 3

1. Claire Gaudiani, *The Greater Good: How Philanthropy Drives The American Economy and Can Save Capitalism* (New York: Time Books, 2003).
2. Mother Teresa, *A Simple Path* (New York: Ballantine Books, 1995).
3. Jimmy Carter, *Living Faith* (New York: Time Books, 1998).

CHAPTER 5

1. Referenced in Richard Boyatzis, Annie McKee, and Daniel Goleman, "Reawakening Your Passion for Work," *Harvard Business Review*, April 2002, 91.

CHAPTER 6

1. Martin Luther King, Jr., *A Call to Conscience: The Landmark Speeches of Dr. Martin Luther King, Jr.* (New York: Warner Books, 2001), 145-146.

CHAPTER 8

1. Referenced in J. Micheal Crant and Thomas S. Bateman, "Charismatic leadership viewed from above: the impact of proactive personality, *Journal of Organizational Behavior*, **21**, February 1999, 63.

CHAPTER 13

1. Go to http://www.redenvelope.com to send gifts for any occasion.

CHAPTER 16

1. CASA stands for Court Appointed Special Advocate. According to their website: "In the United States over one half million children cannot safely live with their families. A CASA volunteer serves an abused or neglected child." You can learn more about CASA by visiting: www.nationalcasa.org/. A brief history of CASA is also taken directly from their website:

    Concerned over making decisions about abused and neglected children's lives without sufficient information, a Seattle judge conceived the idea of using trained community volunteers to speak for the best interests of these children in court. So successful was this Seattle program that soon judges across the country began utilizing citizen advocates. In 1990, the U.S. Congress encouraged the expansion of CASA with passage of the Victims of Child Abuse Act. Today more than 900 CASA programs are in operation, with 70,000 women and men serving as CASA volunteers. CASA is an acronym for Court Appointed Special Advocate.

CHAPTER 20

1. *The Character Institute was founded by Dr. Will Keim and Curtis Zimmerman to educate professionals and students to be character driven leaders who make ethical decisions, handle conflict interpersonally, and have personal responsibility for the choices they make and the consequences of those choices. For more information visit: www.thecharacterinstitute.com.*

CHAPTER 21

1. Jay A. Conger, Rabindra N. Kanungo, and Sanjay T. Menon, "Charismatic leadership and follower effects," *Journal of Organizational Behavior*, **21**, 2000, 747-767.

CHAPTER 22

1. Steve Allen, "*How to Be Funny*," (New York: Prometheus Books, 1998), 57.

CHAPTER 23

1. Fred Rogers, "*The World According to Mister Rogers: Important Things to Remember*," (New York: Hyperion, 2003), 183.
2. Warren G. Bennis and Robert J. Thomas, "*Geeks & Geezers*," (Boston: Harvard Business School Press, 2002), 20. Neoteny is defined as the "retention of youthful qualities by adults."

BIBLIOGRAPHY

Allen, Steve. *How to Be Funny: Discovering the Comic in You.* New York: Prometheus Books, 1998.

Allesandra, Tony. *Charisma.* New York: Warner Books, 1998.

Bennis, Warren G. and Robert J. Thomas. *Geeks and Geezers: How Era, Values, and Defining Moments Shape Leaders.* Boston: Harvard Business School Press, 2002.

Buckingham, Marcus and Donald O. Clifton, Ph.D. *Now, Discover Your Strengths.* New York: The Free Press, 2001.

Buckingham, Marcus and Curt Coffman. *First, Break All The Rules.* New York: Simon & Schuster, 1999.

Chopra, Deepak. *The Seven Spiritual Laws of Success.* California: Amber-Allen Press, 1994.

Carnegie, Dale. *Lifetime Plan for Success.* New York: Galahad Books, 1984.

Carter, Jimmy. *Living Faith.* New York: Random House, 1998.

Covey, Stephen R. *The 7 Habits of Highly Effective People.* New York: Simon & Schuster, 1989.

Darling, Diane. *The Networking Survival Guide: Get the Success You Want by Tapping into the People You Know.* New York: McGraw-Hill, 2003.

Gardner, John W. *On Leadership.* New York: The Free Press, 1990.

Gaudiani, Claire. *The Greater Good: How Philanthropy Drives the American Economy and Can Save Capitalism.* New York: Time Books, 2003.

George, Elizabeth. *Life Management for Busy Women: Living Out God's Plan with Passion and Purpose.* Oregon: Harvest House Publishers, 2002.

Glickman, Ph.D, Rosalene. *Optimal Thinking.* New York: John Wiley & Sons, Inc., 2002.

Hall, Doug. *Jump Start Your Brain.* New York: Warner Books, 1995.

Harrell, Keith. *Attitude is Everything: 10 Life-Changing Steps to Turning Attitude into Action.* New York: HarperCollins Publishers, 2003.

King, Jr., Ph.D., Martin Luther. *A Call to Conscience: The Landmark Speeches of Dr. Martin Luther King, Jr.* New York: Warner Books, 2001.

Loehr, Jim and Tony Schwartz. *The Power of Full Engagement*. New York: Free Press.

Lundin, Ph.D., Stephen C., John Christensen and Harry Paul. *Fish! For Life*. New York: Hyperion Books. 2003

Lama, His Holiness The Dali. *The Art of Happiness: A Handbook for Living*. New York: Riverhead Books. 1998.

Maxwell, John C. *The 21 Irrefutable Laws of Leadership*. Nashville, TN: Thomas Nelson, Inc., 1998.

Nelson, Bob. *1001 Ways to Reward Employees*. New York: Workman Publishing, 1994.

O'Neil, William J. *Business Leaders & Success*. New York: McGraw-Hill, 2004.

Peck, M.D., M. Scott. *Further Along The Road Less Traveled*. New York: Simon & Schuster, 1993.

Roane, Susan. *How to Work a Room*. New York: HarperCollins Publishing, 2002.

Robbins, Anthony. *Awaken The Giant Within*. New York: Simon & Schuster, 1991.

Rogers, Fred. *The World According to Mister Rogers*. New York: Hyperion, 2003.

Sample, Steven B. *The Contrarian's Guide to Leadership*. California: Jossey-Bass, 2002.

Tannen, Deborah. *The Argument Culture: Moving From Debate to Dialogue*. New York: Random House, 1998.

Theresa, Mother. *A Simple Path*. New York: Ballatine Books, 1995.

Tracy, Brian. *Create Your Own Future: How to Master the 12 Critical Factors of Unlimited Success*. New York: John Wiley & Sons, Inc., 2002.

Urban, Hal. *Life's Greatest Lessons: 20 Things That Matter*. New York: Simon & Schuster, 2003.

ABOUT THE AUTHOR

Nancy Hunter Denney is a nationally recognized author and inspirational educator with a passion for life and leadership. In 1993, after living everyone else's definition of having it all, she resigned from administrative duties at a private engineering college to raise her own children, spend more time with her husband, start her own speaking business, and pursue her true passions in life. Nancy specializes in inspiring those who make a difference, especially non-profit helping organizations and is known for her high energy presentation style, sense of humor and passionate delivery of original content. Her clients include the United States Government, over 600 institutions of higher education, Deloitte-Touche, Century 21 Real Estate, Junior Leagues, The Biennial Conference for Women, The iWoman Conference, YMCA, and numerous national professional associations. Her goal in life is to encourage others to live their lives in the interested student of life position. Nancy resides (and sails) with her family in Marion, MA.

For more information:
Call: 888.566.7536
Visit: **www.nancyhunterdenney.com** (includes on-line store)
www.zingbook.com
Write: Nancy Hunter Denney
Box 1041
Marion, MA 02738

BOOKS AND PRODUCTS

BY NANCY HUNTER DENNEY

Life by Design: A Do-It-Yourself Approach to Achieving Happiness
Let Your Leadership Speak: How to Lead and Be Heard

CD: "The Voice of Charisma"

Video: *The Future is Yours to Create* video – a seven minute collection of inspirational clips on time, love, life, leadership, and freedom.

Inspirational Products: Posters, coffee mugs and T-shirts

GO TO: Nancy's **on-line store** at **www.nancyhunterdenney.com**
or call 888-566-7536.

THANK YOU FOR MAKING A DIFFERENCE!
Partial proceeds from the sale of *Zing!* benefit the community
resources found in Appendix B.